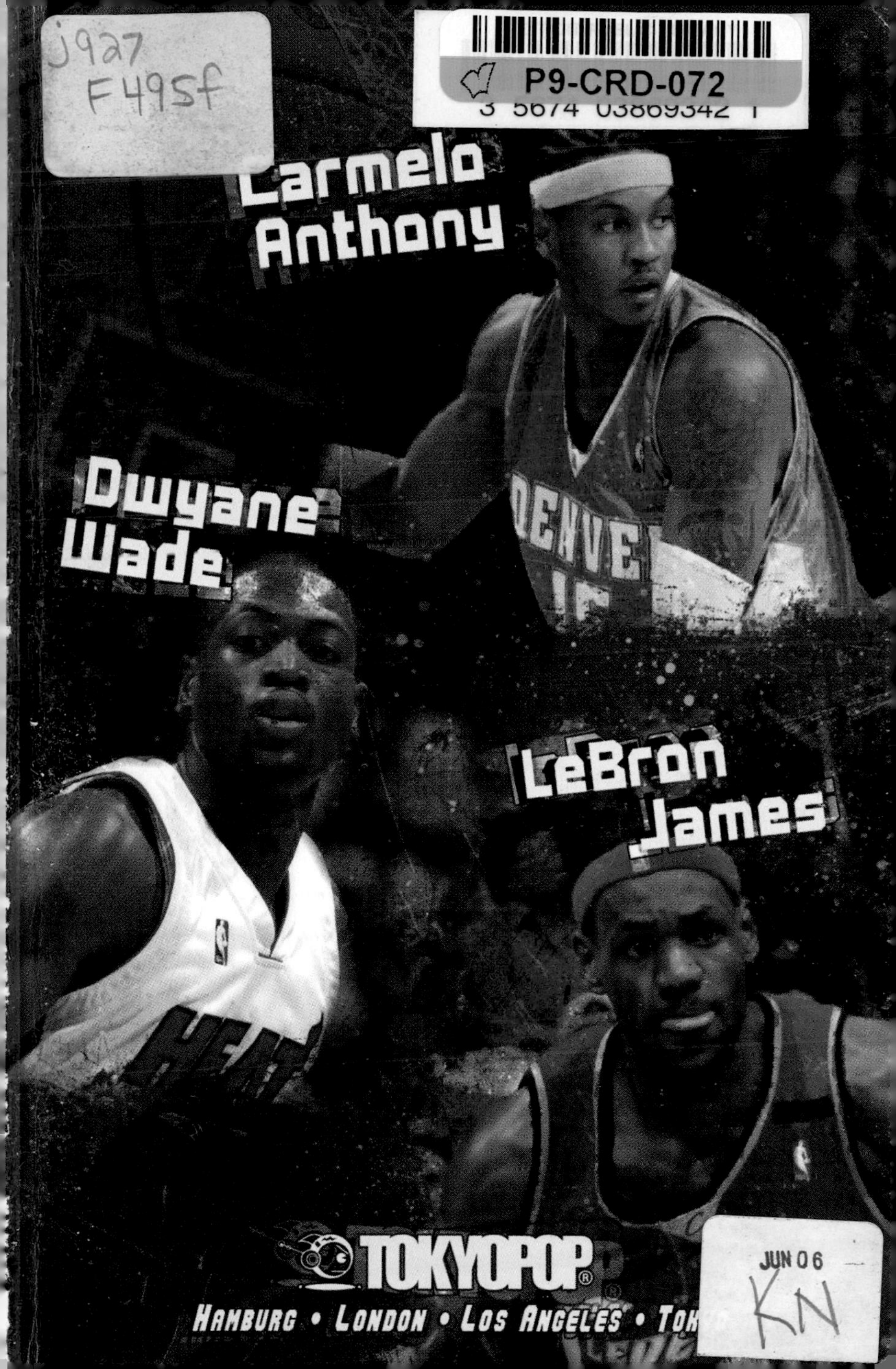
Carmelo
Anthony
DENVER
Dwyane
Wade
HEAT
LeBron
James
TOKYOPOP
HAMBURG • LONDON • LOS ANGELES • TOK

Editor - Zachary Rau
Graphic Designer and Letterer - Anna Kernbaum
Cover Designer - Tomas Montalvo-Lagos
Illustrations - Tomas Montalvo-Lagos
Inking - Tomas Montalvo-Lagos & Chris Tjalsma

Digital Imaging Manager - Chris Buford
Production Managers - Jennifer Miller and Mutsumi Miyazaki
Senior Designer - Anna Kernbaum
Senior Editor - Elizabeth Hurchalla
Managing Editor - Jill Freshney
VP of Production - Ron Klamert
Publisher & Editor-in-Chief - Mike Kiley
President & C.O.O. - John Parker
C.E.O. - Stuart Levy

E-mail: info@TOKYOPOP.com
Come visit us online at www.TOKYOPOP.com

A ⊙ TOKYOPOP® Cine-Manga® Book
TOKYOPOP Inc.
5900 Wilshire Blvd., Suite 2000
Los Angeles, CA 90036

The Future Greatest Stars of the NBA: LeBron James,
Dwyane Wade and Carmelo Anthony

ISBN: 1-59532-894-7

First TOKYOPOP® printing: November 2005

10 9 8 7 6 5 4 3 2 1

Printed in Canada

GREATEST STARS OF THE NBA

NBA

Written by
Jon Finkel

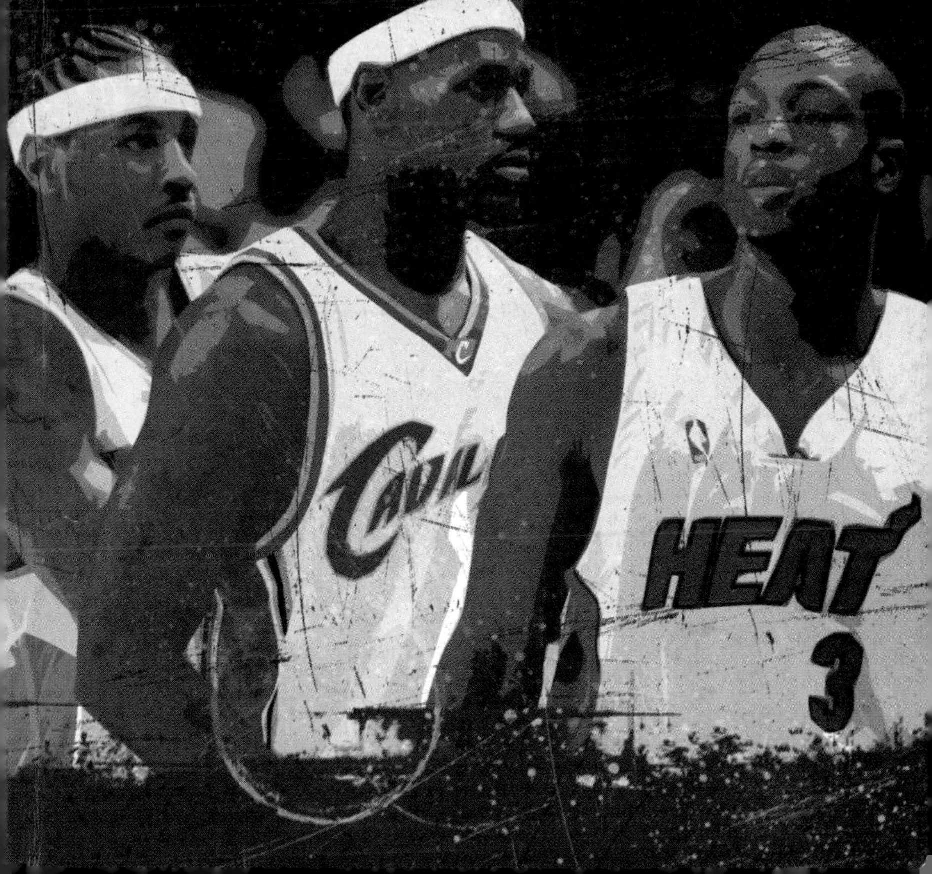
HEAT
3

CONTENTS://

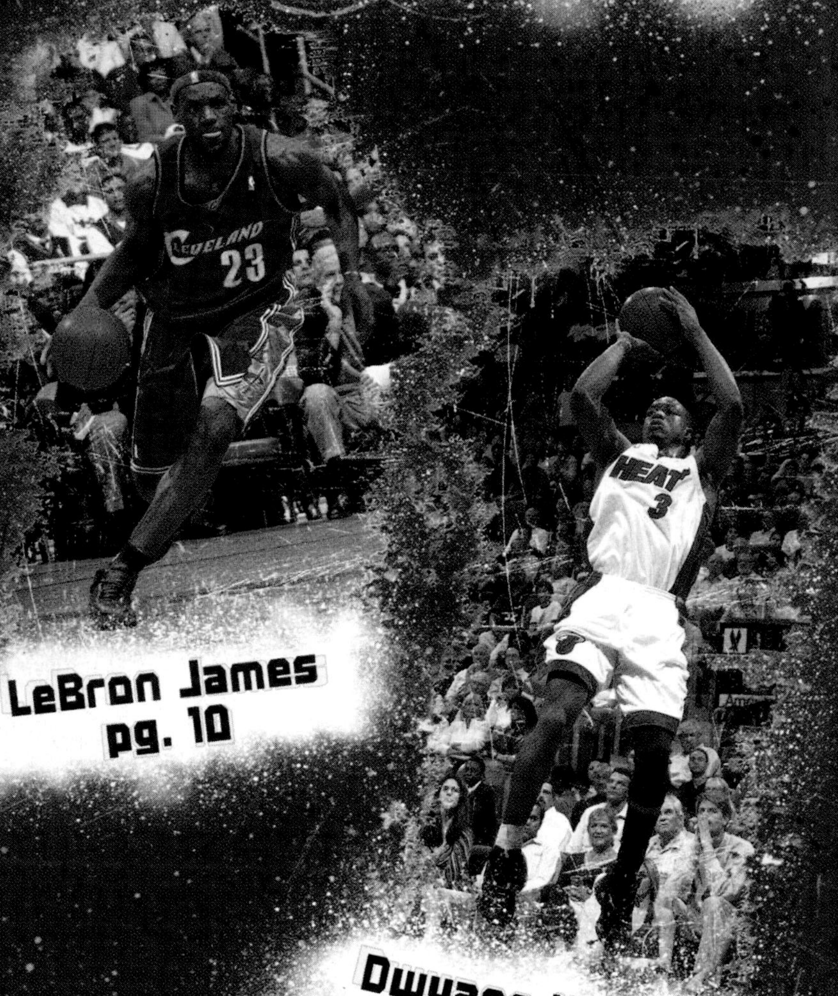

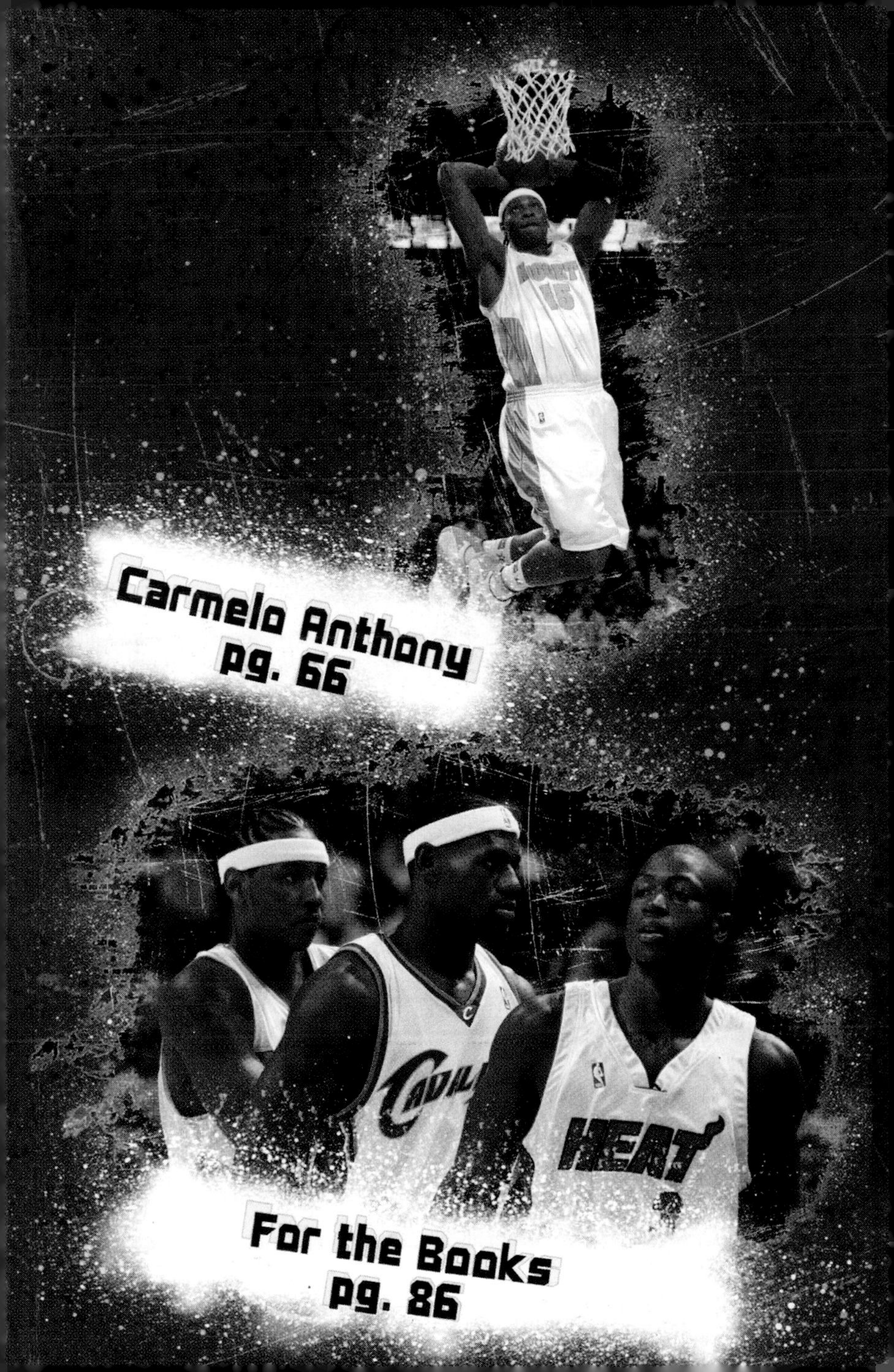
Carmelo Anthony
pg. 66
For the Books
pg. 86

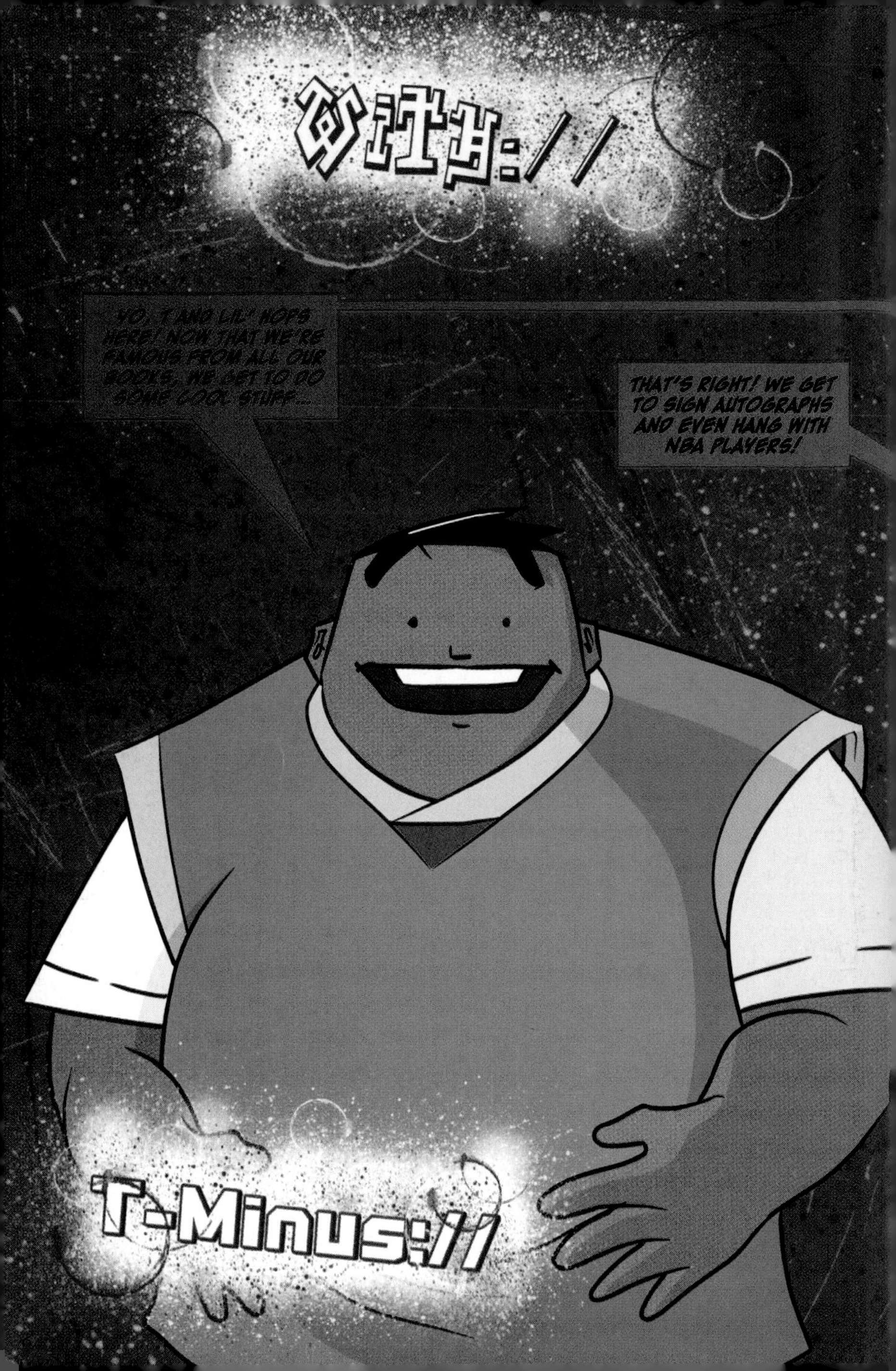
WITH://
YO, T AND LIL' HOPS HERE! NOW THAT WE'RE FAMOUS FROM ALL OUR BOOKS, WE GET TO DO SOME COOL STUFF...
THAT'S RIGHT! WE GET TO SIGN AUTOGRAPHS AND EVEN HANG WITH NBA PLAYERS!
T-Minus://

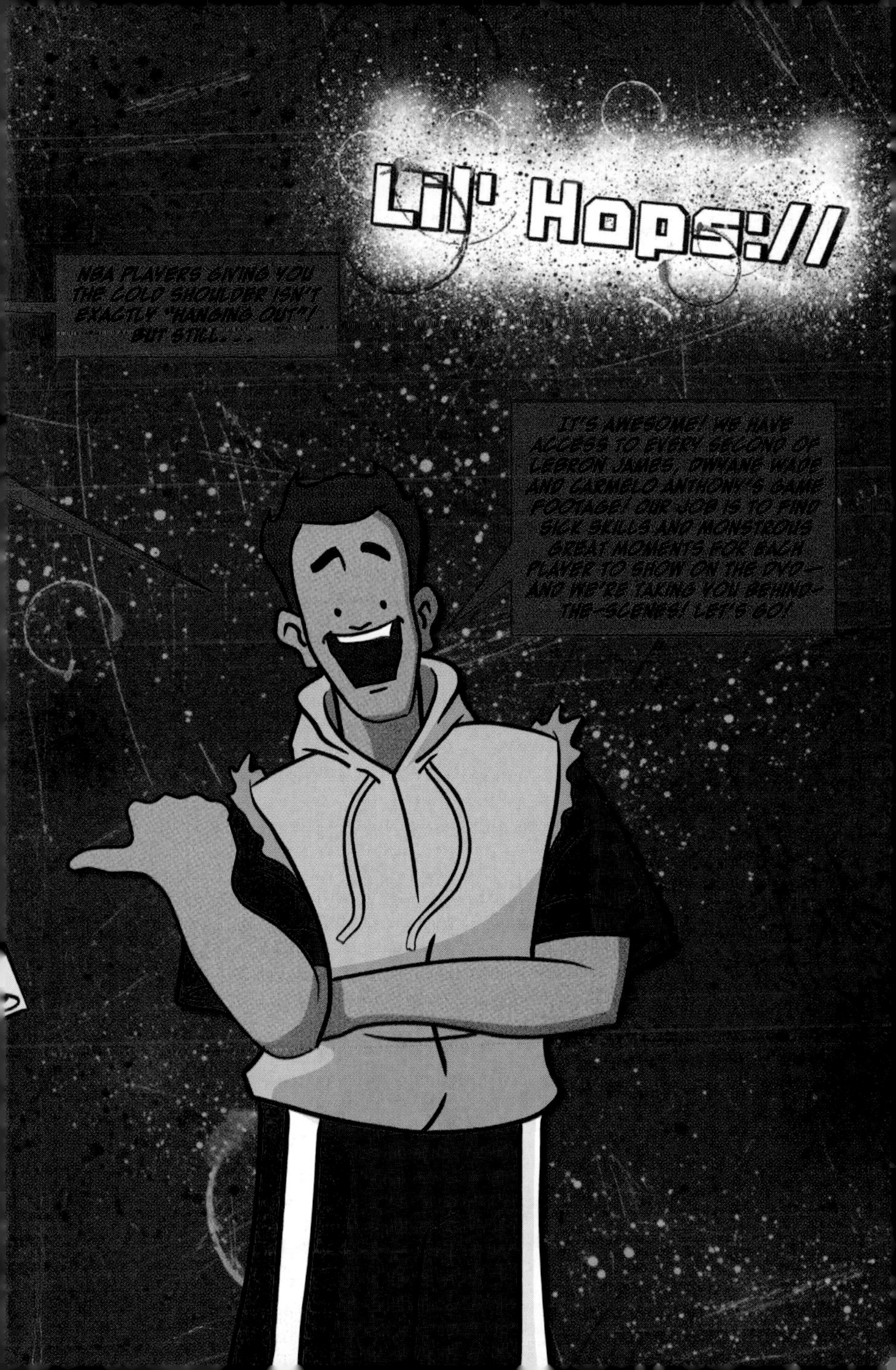
Lil' Hops://
NBA PLAYERS GIVING YOU THE COLD SHOULDER ISN'T EXACTLY "HANGING OUT"! BUT STILL...
IT'S AWESOME! WE HAVE ACCESS TO EVERY SECOND OF LEBRON JAMES, DWYANE WADE AND CARMELO ANTHONY'S GAME FOOTAGE! OUR JOB IS TO FIND SICK SKILLS AND MONSTROUS GREAT MOMENTS FOR EACH PLAYER TO SHOW ON THE DVD—AND WE'RE TAKING YOU BEHIND-THE-SCENES! LET'S GO!

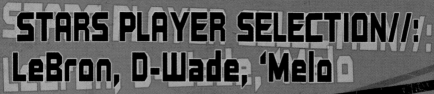

STARS PLAYER SELECTION//: LeBron, D-Wade, 'Melo

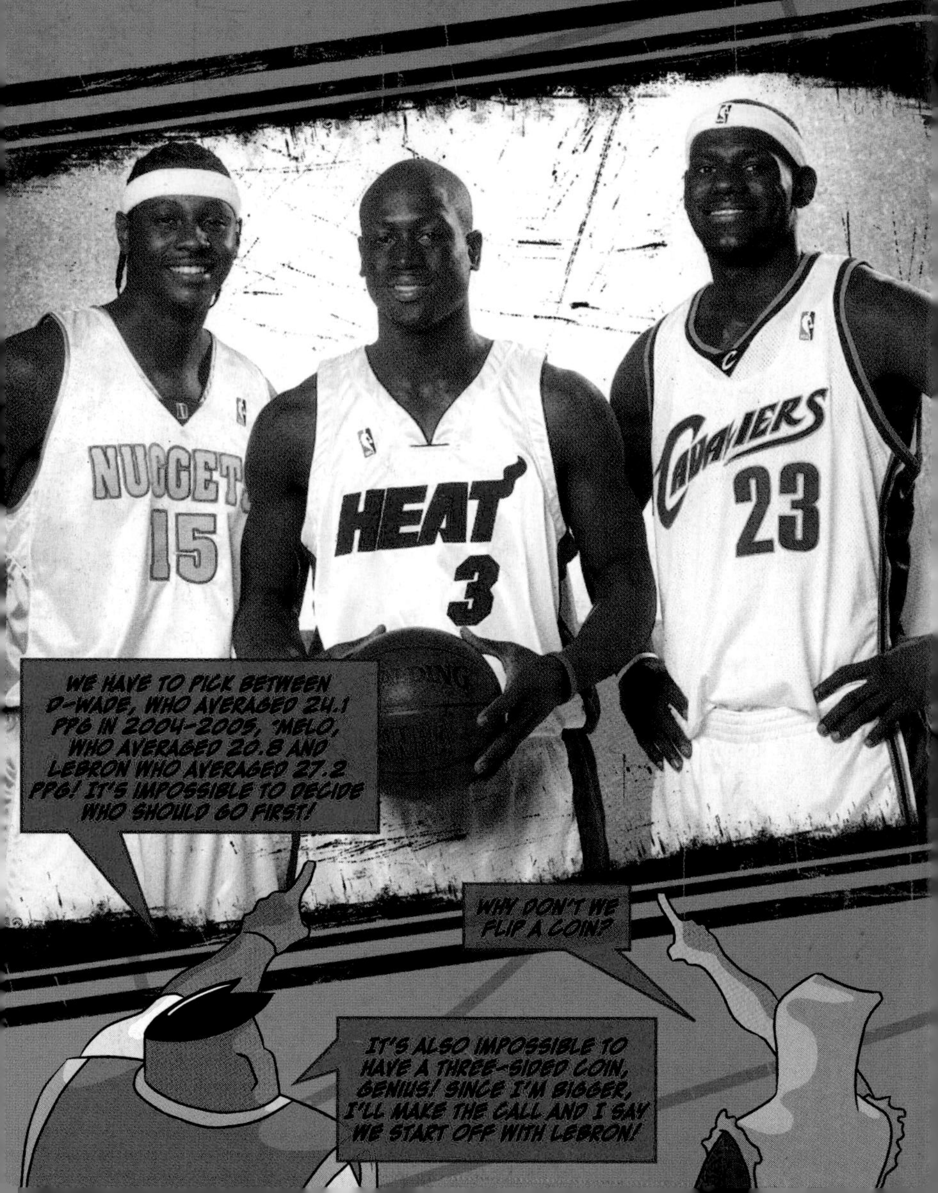
NUGGETS 15
HEAT 3
CAVALIERS 23
WE HAVE TO PICK BETWEEN D-WADE, WHO AVERAGED 24.1 PPG IN 2004-2005, 'MELO, WHO AVERAGED 20.8 AND LEBRON WHO AVERAGED 27.2 PPG! IT'S IMPOSSIBLE TO DECIDE WHO SHOULD GO FIRST!
WHY DON'T WE FLIP A COIN?
IT'S ALSO IMPOSSIBLE TO HAVE A THREE-SIDED COIN, GENIUS! SINCE I'M BIGGER, I'LL MAKE THE CALL AND I SAY WE START OFF WITH LEBRON!

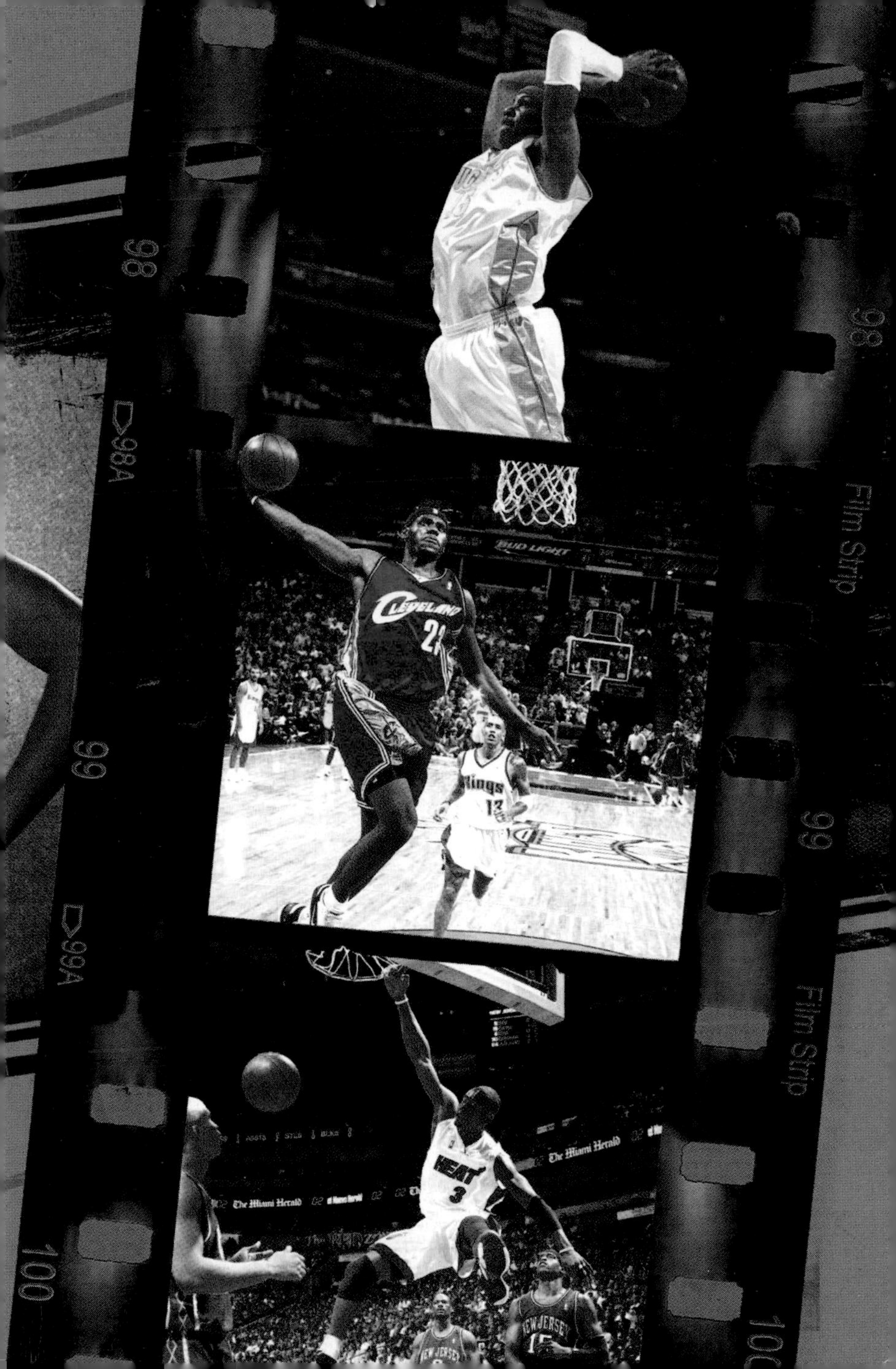
Film Strip
98
98A
99
99A
100
CLEVELAND
23
Kings
12
BUD LIGHT
HEAT
3
The Miami Herald
NEW JERSEY
15

PLAYER SELECTED//: LEBRON JAMES

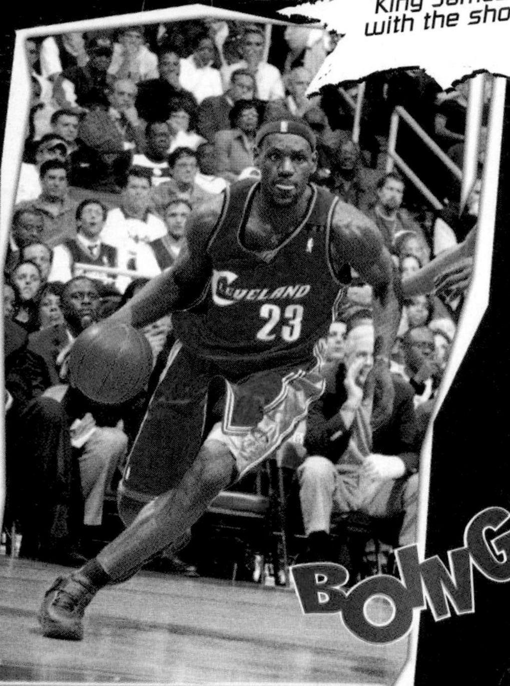
King James with the shot!
BOING!

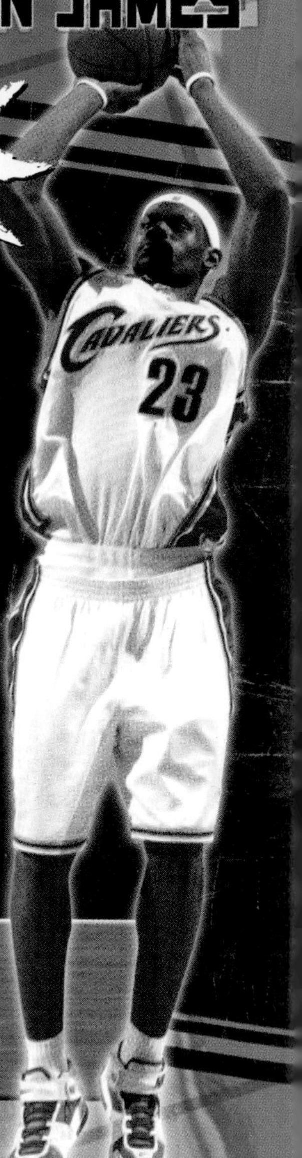

#23 / Guard

Height//: 6' 8"

Weight//: 240

Born//: Akron, Ohio / Dec. 30, 1984

Nicknames//: King James, The Chosen One, The Gift

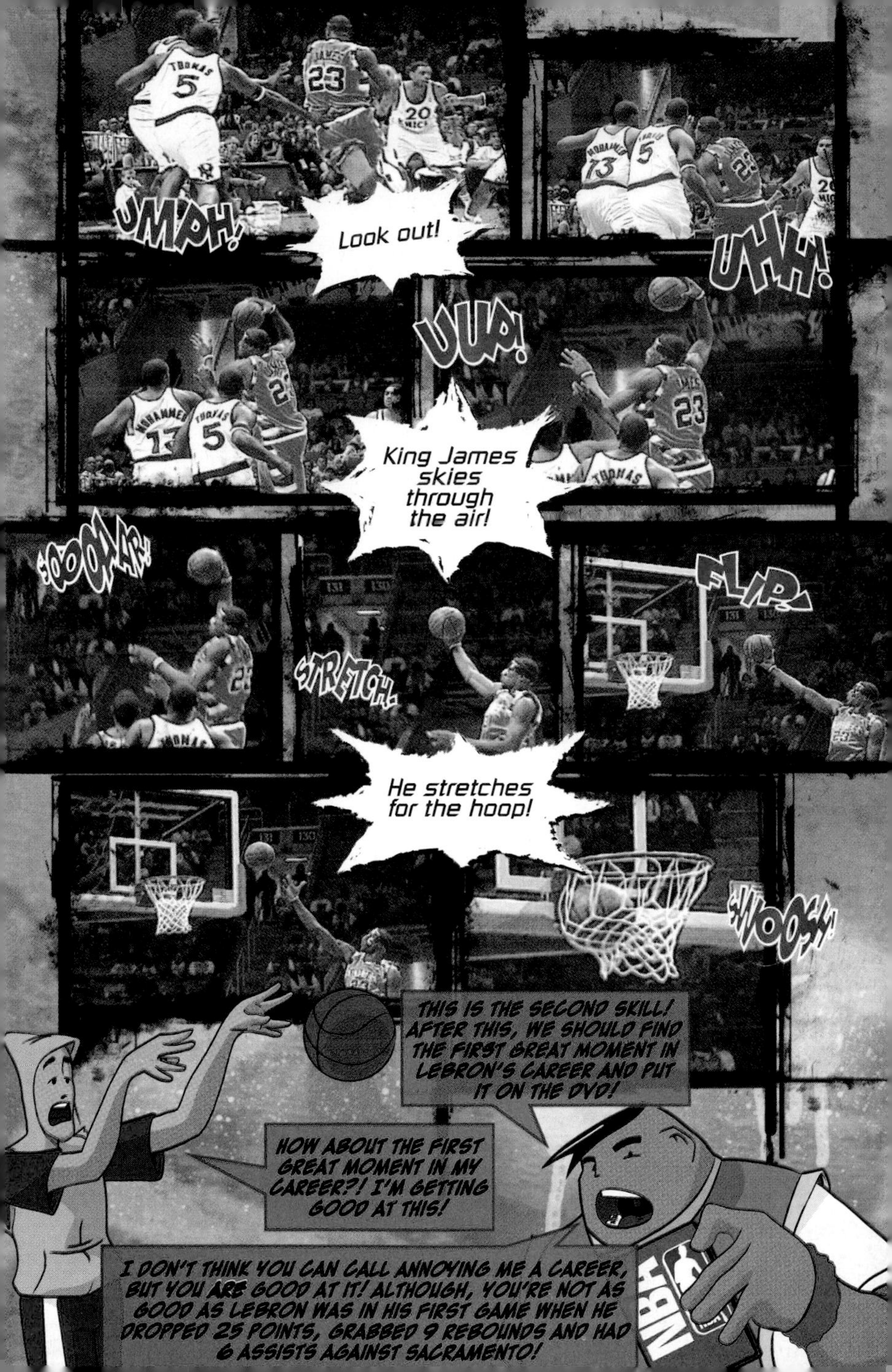
UMPH!
Look out!
UHH!
UUP!
King James skies through the air!
SOOOAR!
STRETCH.
FLIP!
He stretches for the hoop!
SWOOSH!
THIS IS THE SECOND SKILL! AFTER THIS, WE SHOULD FIND THE FIRST GREAT MOMENT IN LEBRON'S CAREER AND PUT IT ON THE DVD!
HOW ABOUT THE FIRST GREAT MOMENT IN MY CAREER?! I'M GETTING GOOD AT THIS!
I DON'T THINK YOU CAN CALL ANNOYING ME A CAREER, BUT YOU ARE GOOD AT IT! ALTHOUGH, YOU'RE NOT AS GOOD AS LEBRON WAS IN HIS FIRST GAME WHEN HE DROPPED 25 POINTS, GRABBED 9 REBOUNDS AND HAD 6 ASSISTS AGAINST SACRAMENTO!

GREAT MOMENT UNLOCKED!

YOUNGEST NBA PLAYER TO SCORE 40 3/27/04!

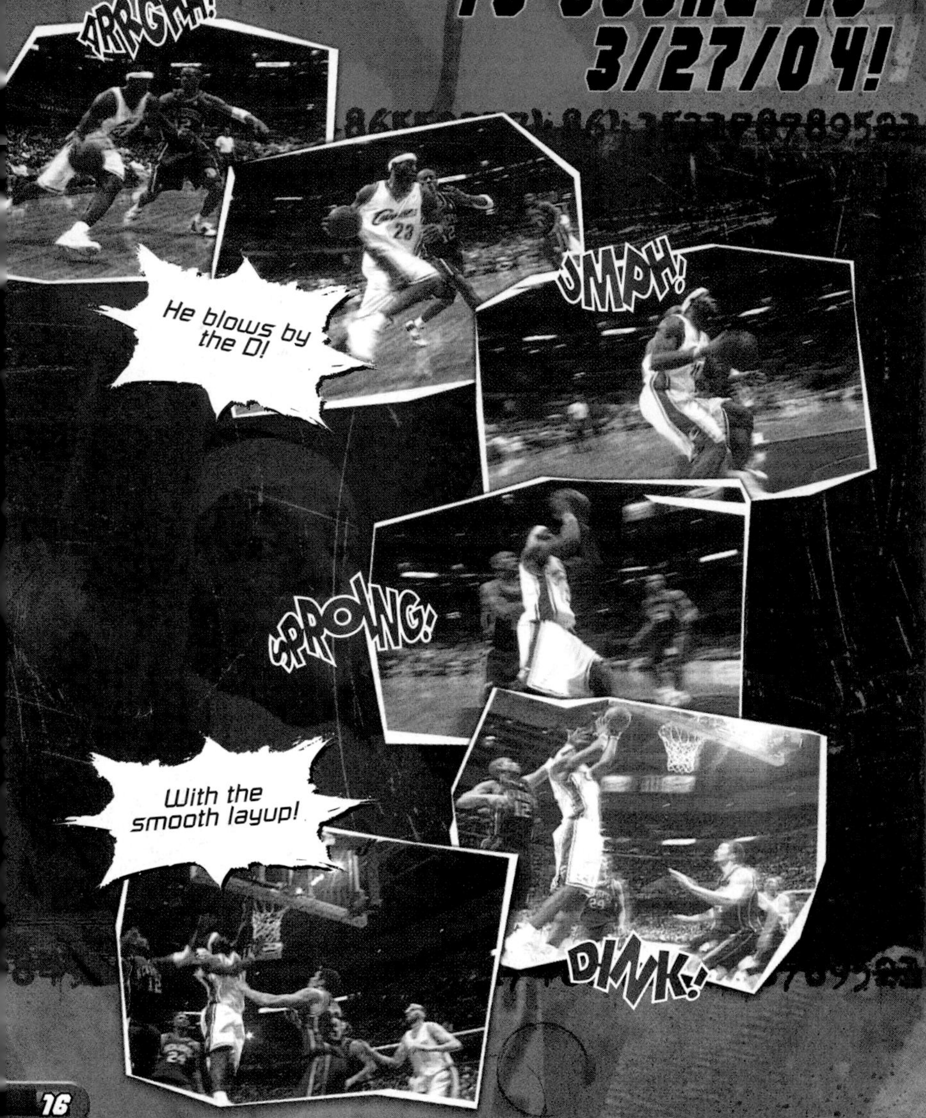

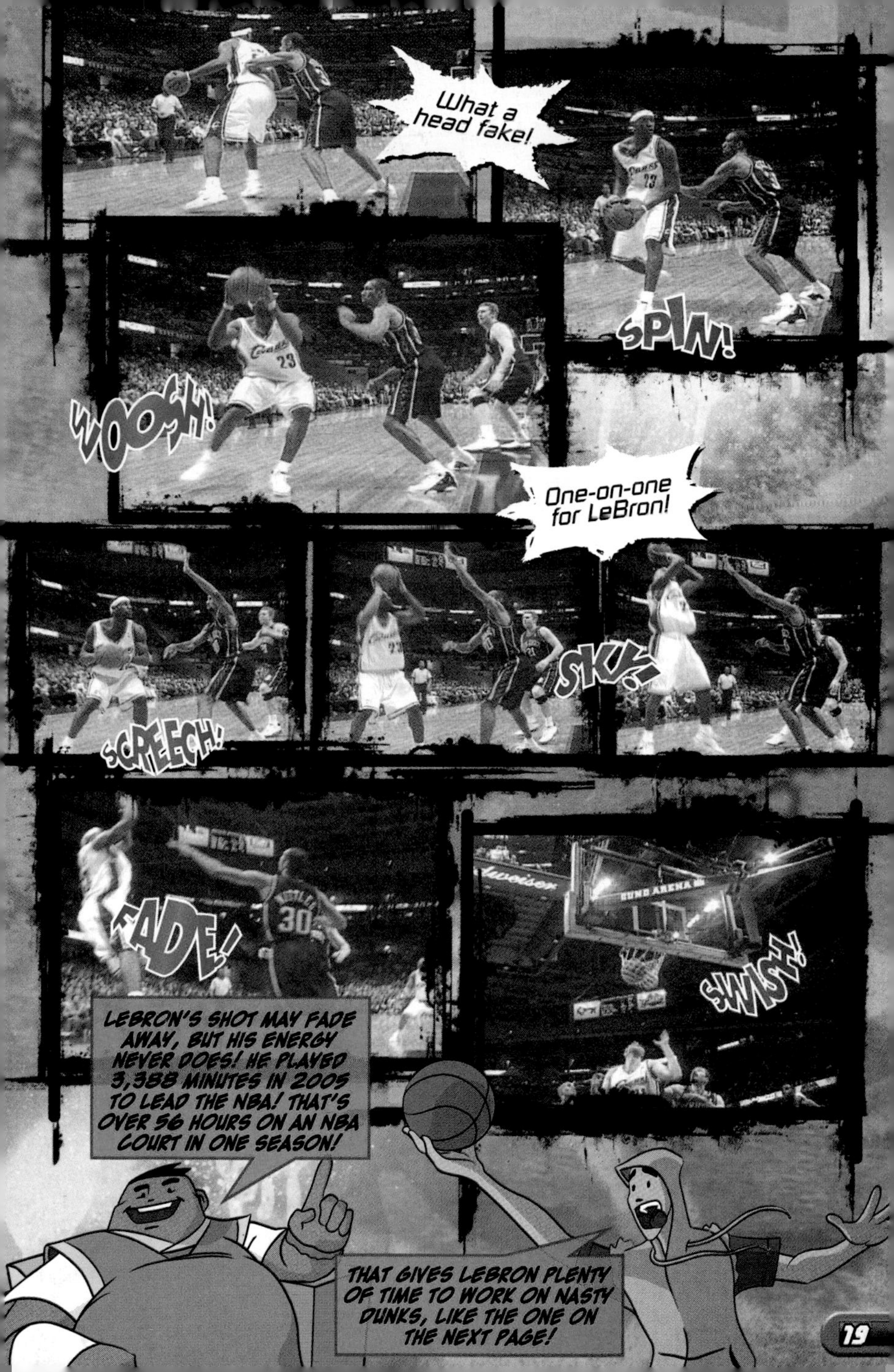
What a head fake!
SPIN!
WOOSH!
One-on-one for LeBron!
SCREECH!
SKY!
FADE!
SWISH!
LEBRON'S SHOT MAY FADE AWAY, BUT HIS ENERGY NEVER DOES! HE PLAYED 3,388 MINUTES IN 2005 TO LEAD THE NBA! THAT'S OVER 56 HOURS ON AN NBA COURT IN ONE SEASON!
THAT GIVES LEBRON PLENTY OF TIME TO WORK ON NASTY DUNKS, LIKE THE ONE ON THE NEXT PAGE!

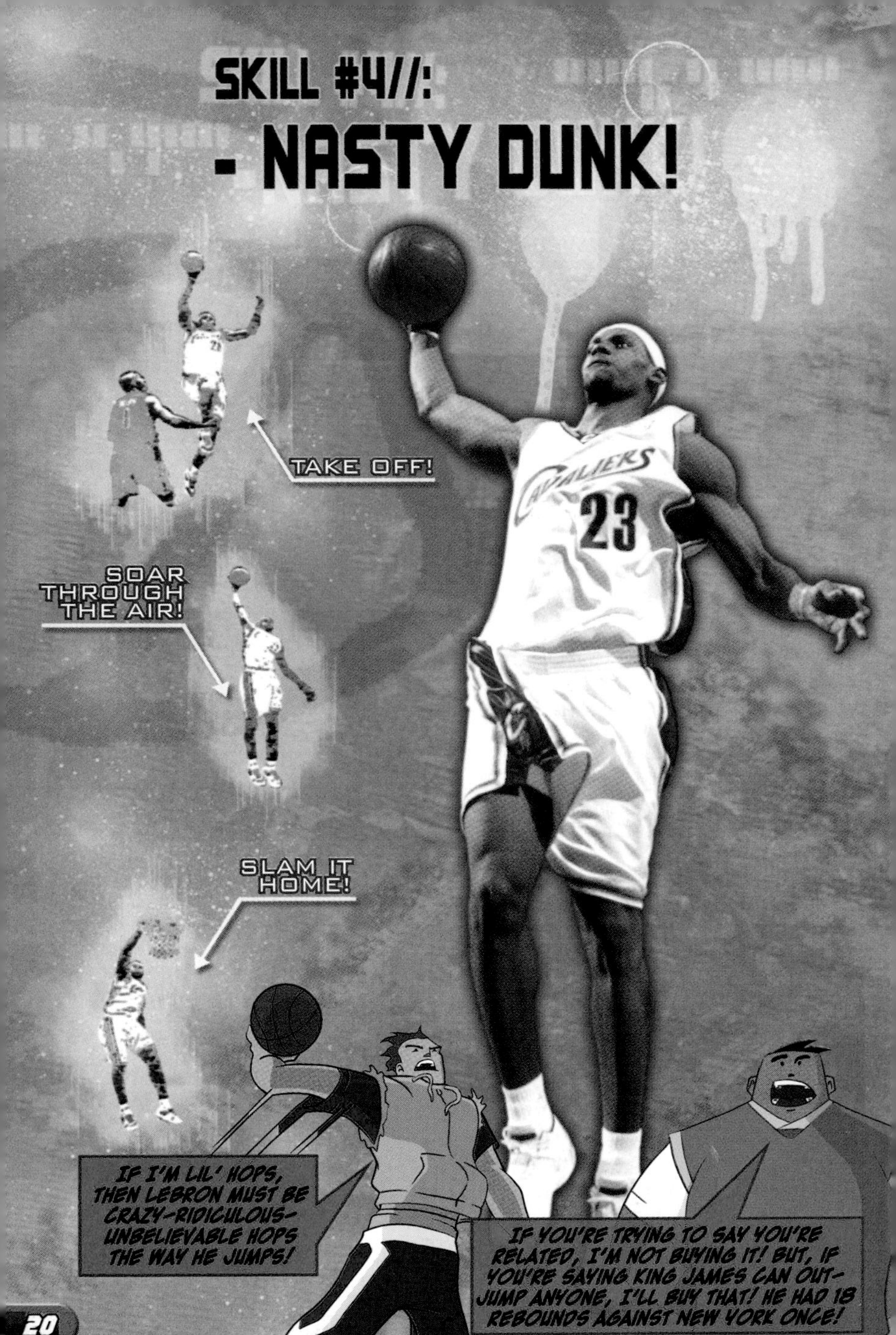
SKILL #4//:
- NASTY DUNK!
TAKE OFF!
SOAR THROUGH THE AIR!
SLAM IT HOME!
23
IF I'M LIL' HOPS, THEN LEBRON MUST BE CRAZY-RIDICULOUS-UNBELIEVABLE HOPS THE WAY HE JUMPS!
IF YOU'RE TRYING TO SAY YOU'RE RELATED, I'M NOT BUYING IT! BUT, IF YOU'RE SAYING KING JAMES CAN OUT-JUMP ANYONE, I'LL BUY THAT! HE HAD 18 REBOUNDS AGAINST NEW YORK ONCE!

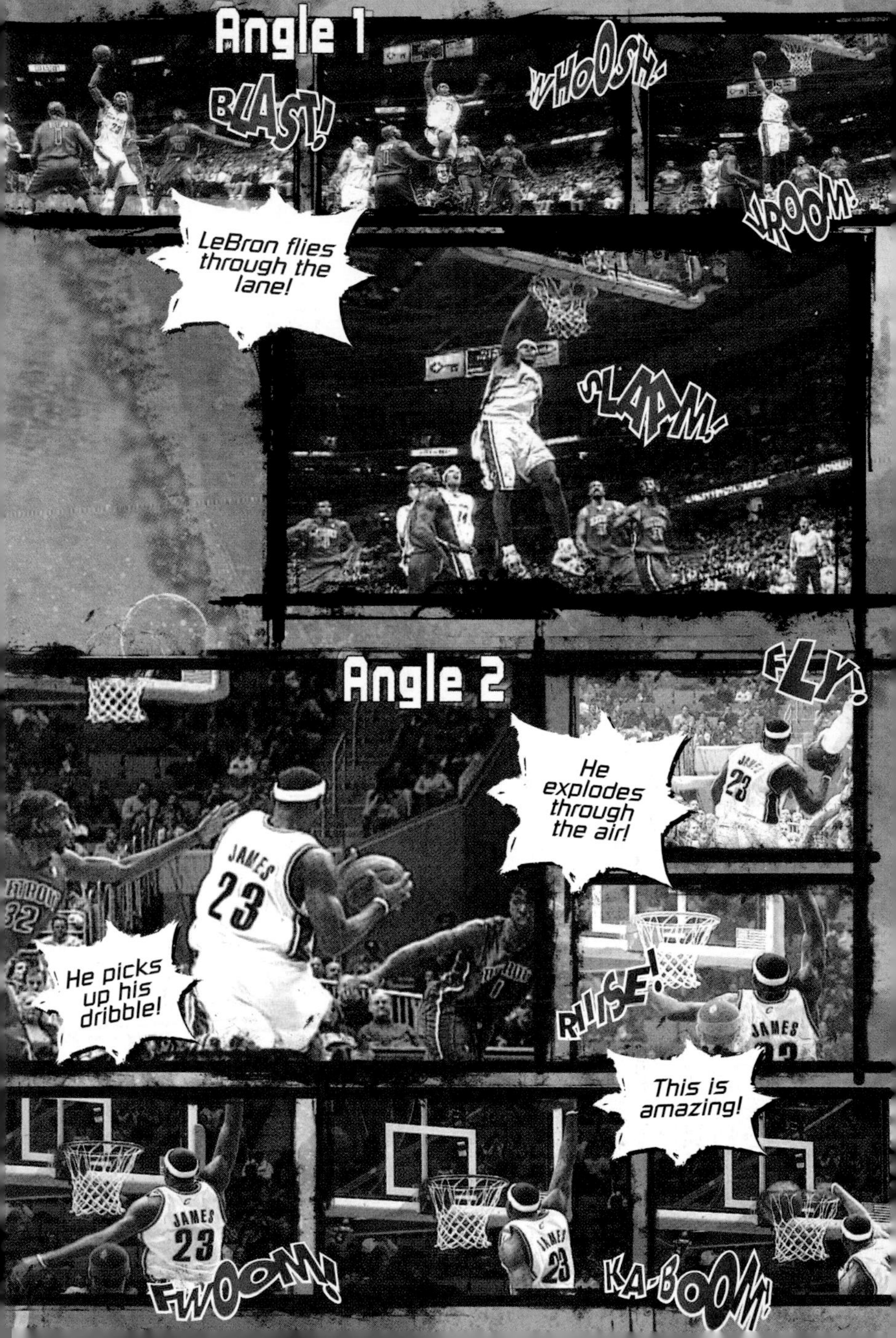
Angle 1
BLAST!
WHOOSH!
VROOM!
LeBron flies through the lane!
SLAAM!
Angle 2
He picks up his dribble!
FLY!
He explodes through the air!
RIISE!
FWOOM!
This is amazing!
KA-BOOM!

SKILL #5//:
- SICK STEAL!

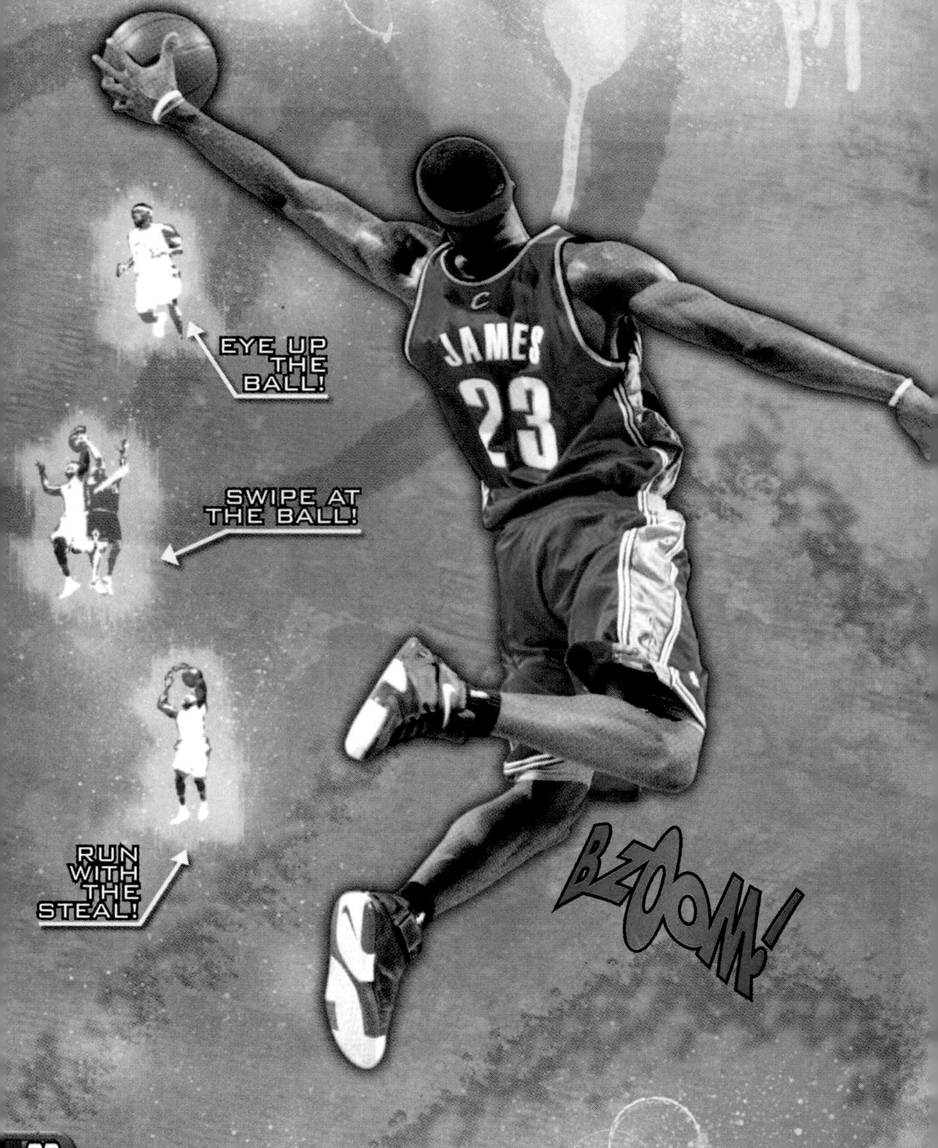

JAMES
23
EYE UP THE BALL!
SWIPE AT THE BALL!
RUN WITH THE STEAL!
BZOOM!

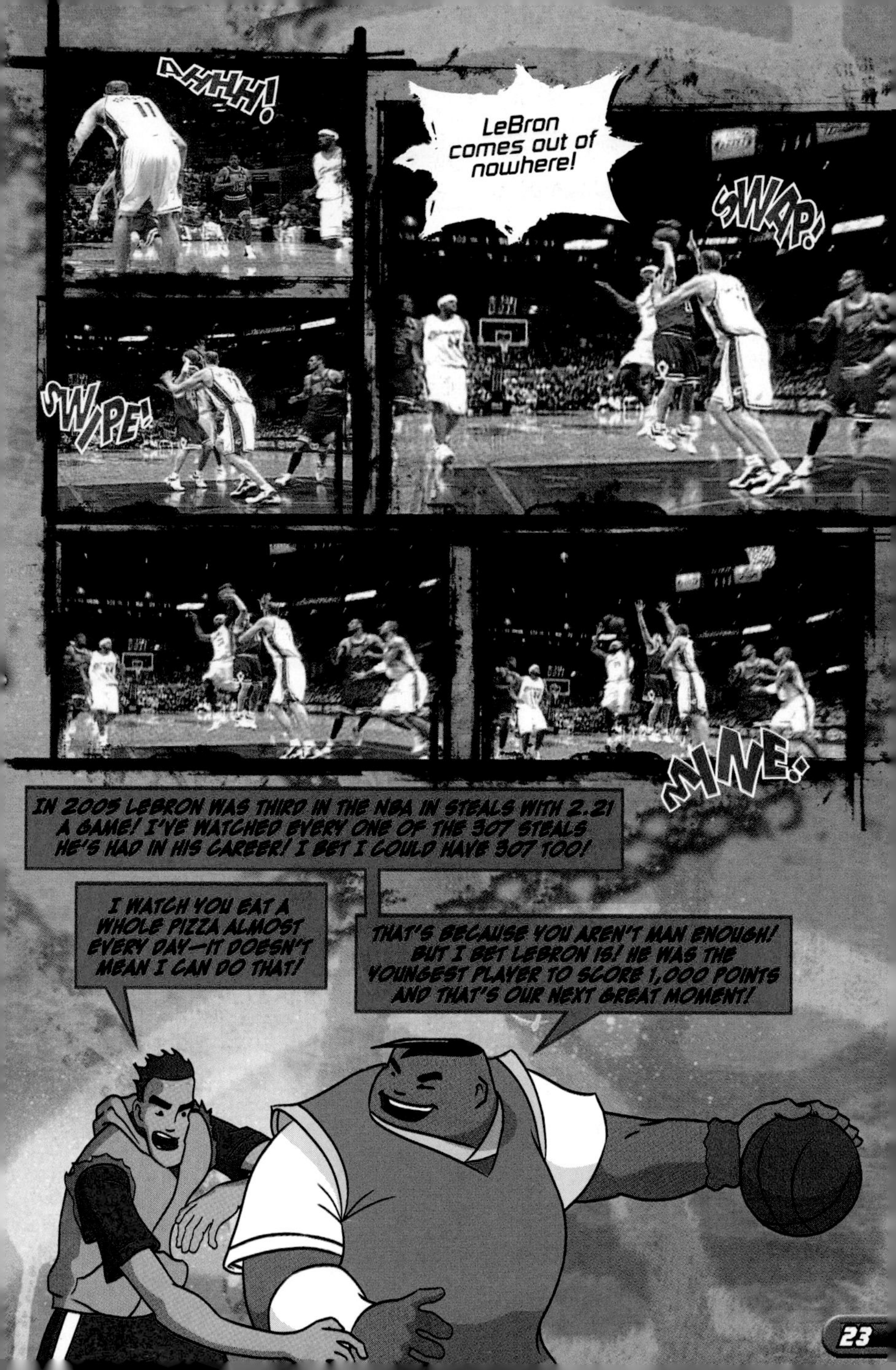
AHHH!
SWIPE!
LeBron comes out of nowhere!
SWAP!
MINE!
IN 2005 LEBRON WAS THIRD IN THE NBA IN STEALS WITH 2.21 A GAME! I'VE WATCHED EVERY ONE OF THE 307 STEALS HE'S HAD IN HIS CAREER! I BET I COULD HAVE 307 TOO!
I WATCH YOU EAT A WHOLE PIZZA ALMOST EVERY DAY—IT DOESN'T MEAN I CAN DO THAT!
THAT'S BECAUSE YOU AREN'T MAN ENOUGH! BUT I BET LEBRON IS! HE WAS THE YOUNGEST PLAYER TO SCORE 1,000 POINTS AND THAT'S OUR NEXT GREAT MOMENT!

GREAT MOMENT UNLOCKED!

YOUNGEST TO SCORE 1,000 2/9/05!

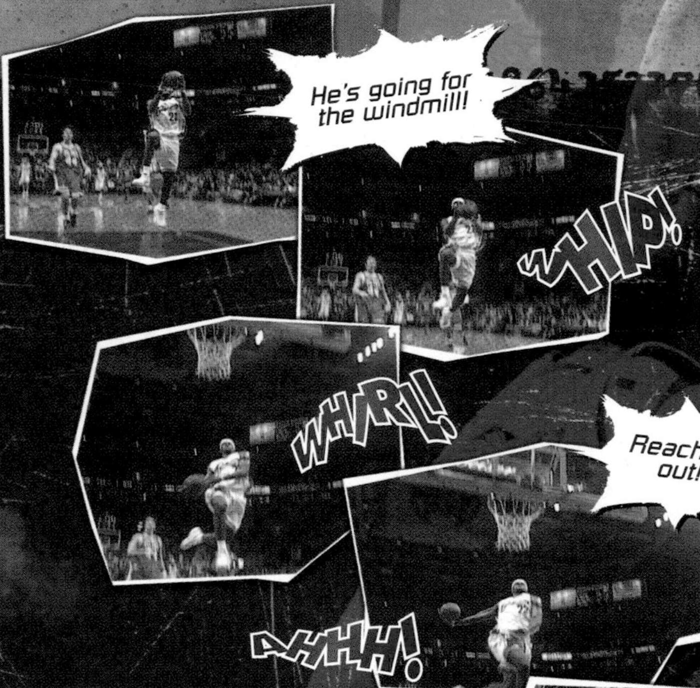
He's going for the windmill!
WHIP!
WHIRL!
Reaches out!
AHHH!

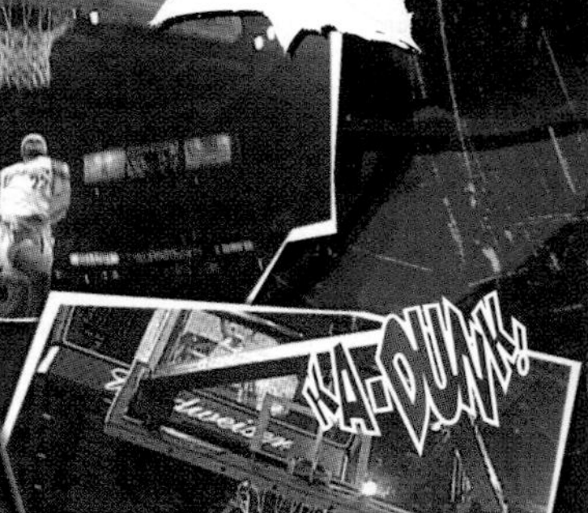
KA-DUNK!

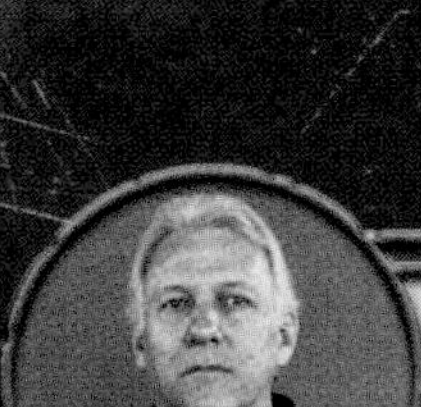

GREGG POPOVICH

SAN ANTONIO SPURS

HEAD COACH

"HIS MATURITY, IN THE SENSE THAT HE REALLY UNDERSTANDS THE RESPONSIBILITY HE HAS AS A BIG-TIME, MONEY BASKETBALL PLAYER TO BRING IT EVERY NIGHT, IS WHAT SETS HIM APART." [2]

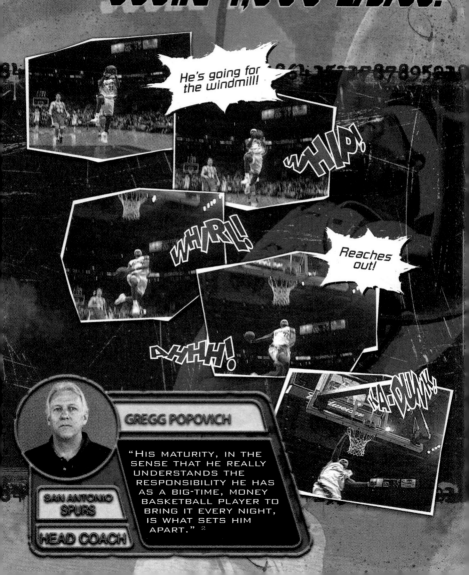

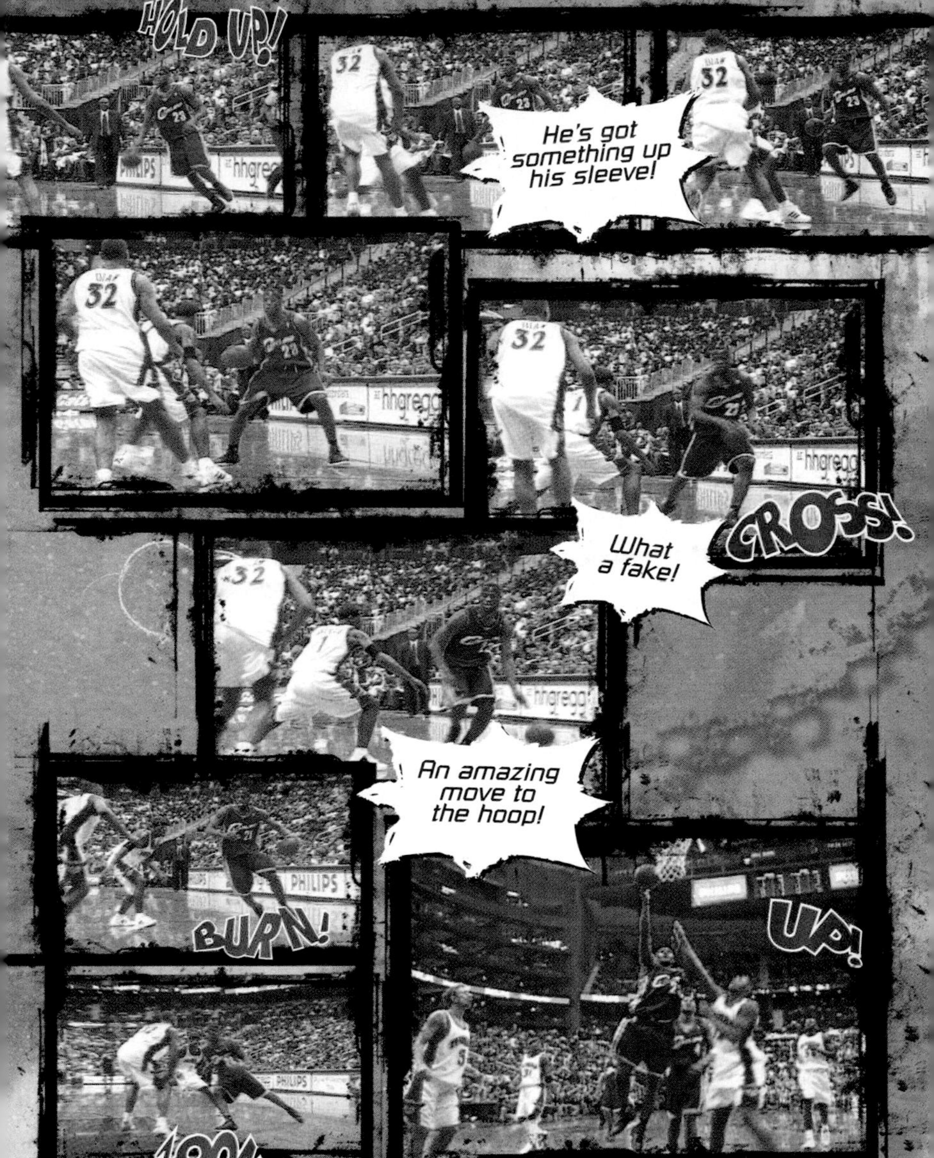
HOLD UP!
He's got something up his sleeve!
What a fake!
CROSS!
An amazing move to the hoop!
BURN!
ZOOM!
UP!

SKILL #8//:
- POWER DUNK!

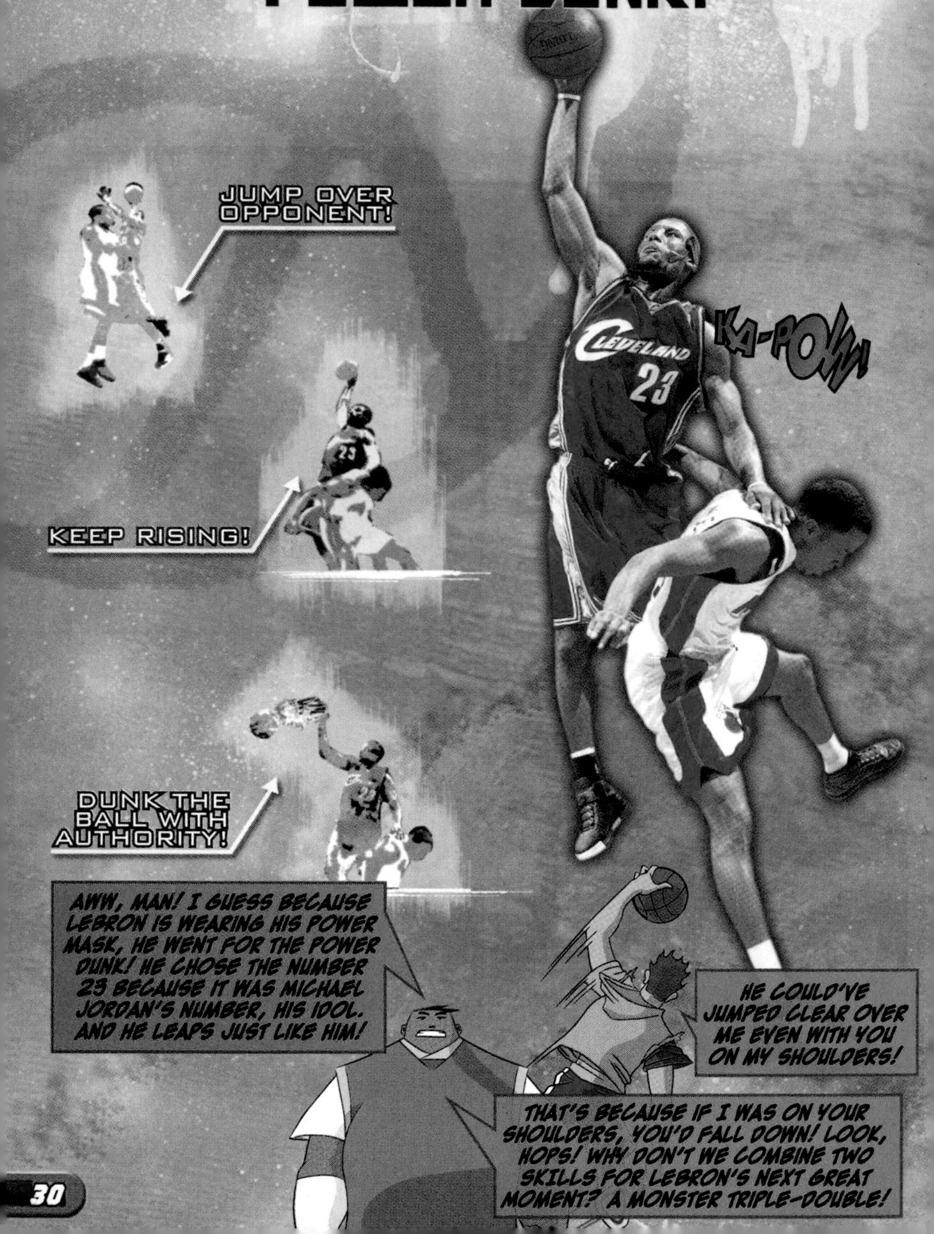
JUMP OVER OPPONENT!
KA-POW!
KEEP RISING!
DUNK THE BALL WITH AUTHORITY!
AWW, MAN! I GUESS BECAUSE LEBRON IS WEARING HIS POWER MASK, HE WENT FOR THE POWER DUNK! HE CHOSE THE NUMBER 23 BECAUSE IT WAS MICHAEL JORDAN'S NUMBER, HIS IDOL. AND HE LEAPS JUST LIKE HIM!
HE COULD'VE JUMPED CLEAR OVER ME EVEN WITH YOU ON MY SHOULDERS!
THAT'S BECAUSE IF I WAS ON YOUR SHOULDERS, YOU'D FALL DOWN! LOOK, HOPS! WHY DON'T WE COMBINE TWO SKILLS FOR LEBRON'S NEXT GREAT MOMENT? A MONSTER TRIPLE-DOUBLE!

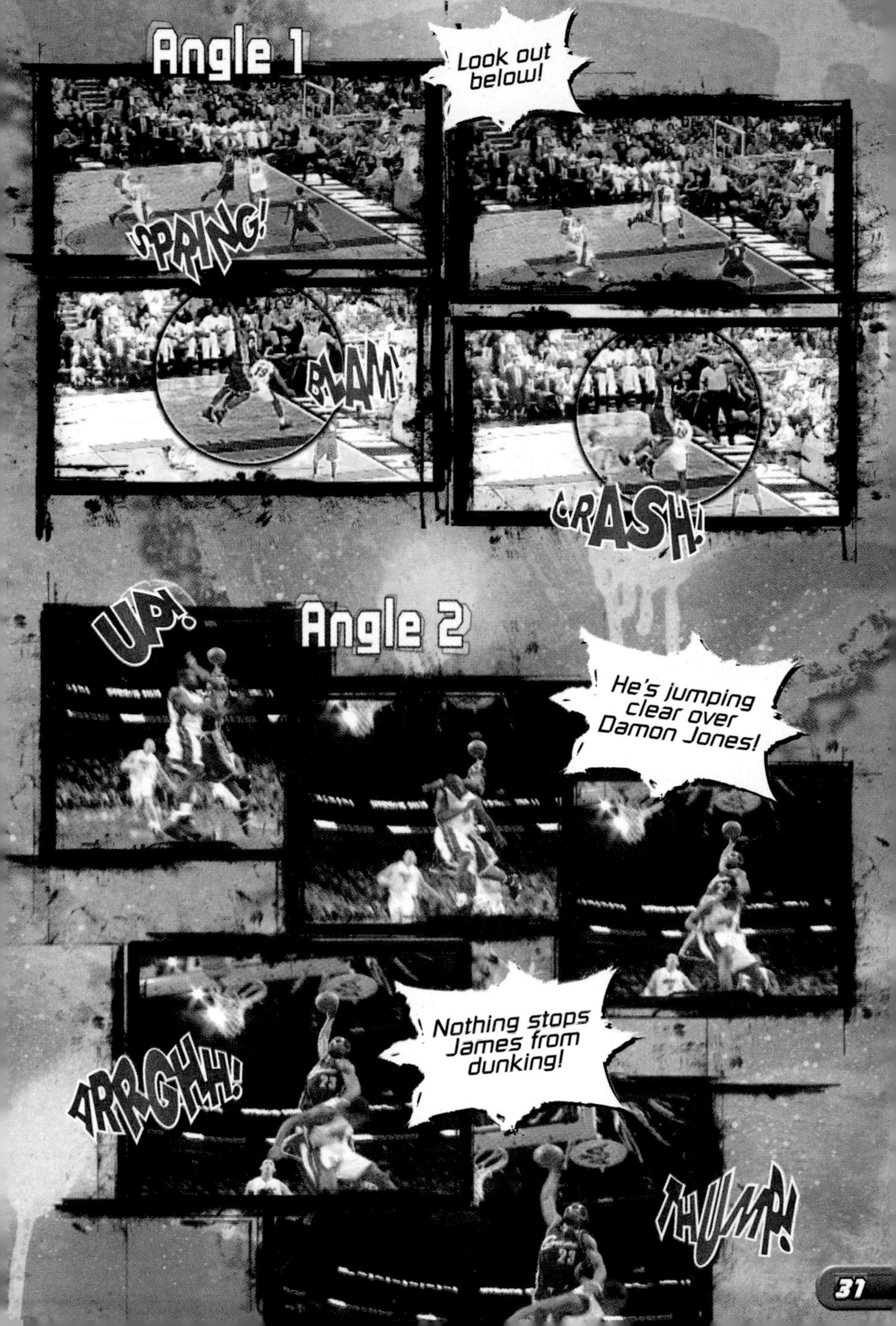

Angle 1
SPRING!
Look out below!
BLAM!
CRASH!
Angle 2
UP!
He's jumping clear over Damon Jones!
ARRGHH!
Nothing stops James from dunking!
THUMP!

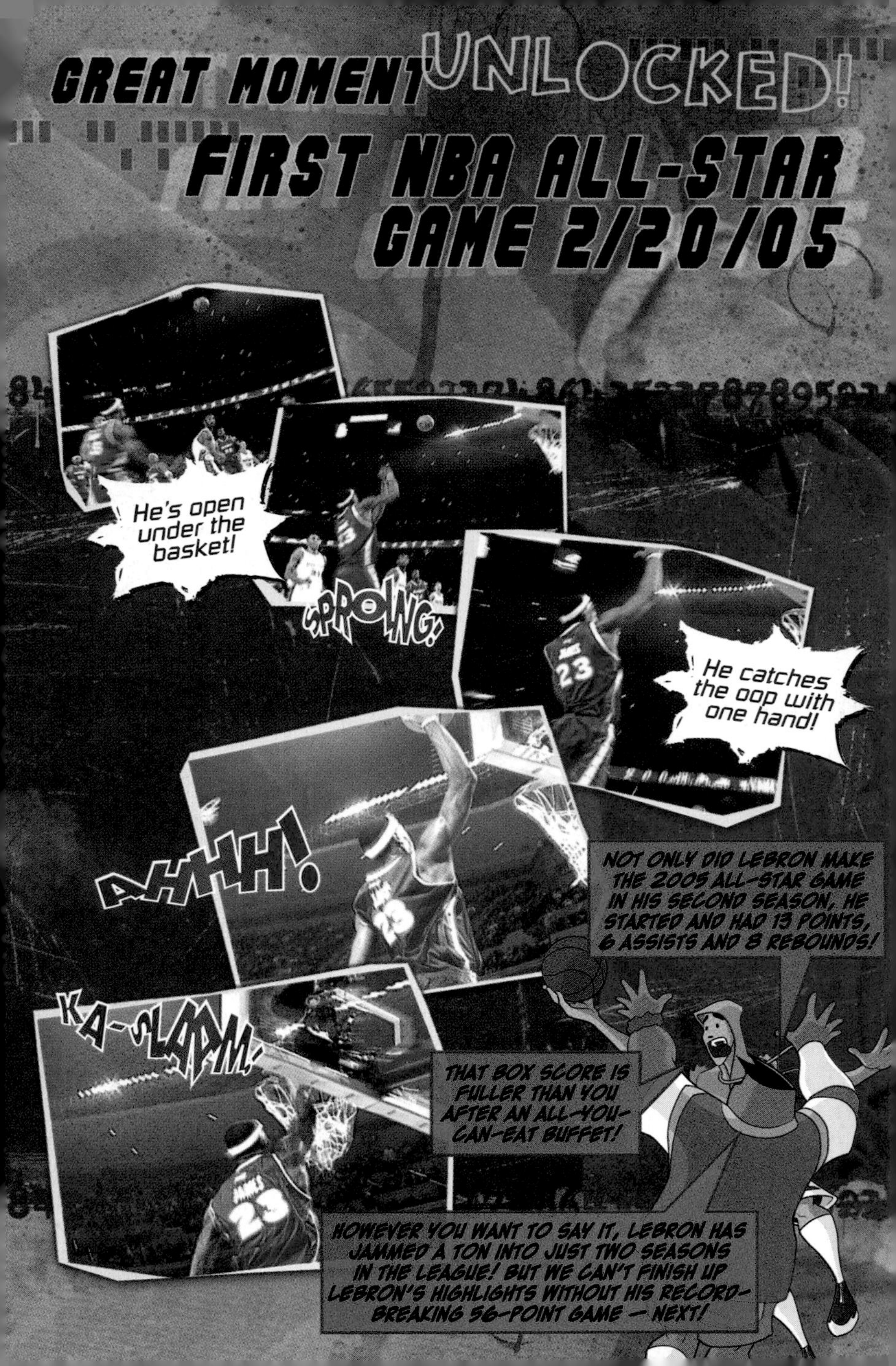
GREAT MOMENT UNLOCKED!
FIRST NBA ALL-STAR GAME 2/20/05
He's open under the basket!
SPROING!
He catches the oop with one hand!
AHHHH!
NOT ONLY DID LEBRON MAKE THE 2005 ALL-STAR GAME IN HIS SECOND SEASON, HE STARTED AND HAD 13 POINTS, 6 ASSISTS AND 8 REBOUNDS!
KA-SLAMM!
THAT BOX SCORE IS FULLER THAN YOU AFTER AN ALL-YOU-CAN-EAT BUFFET!
HOWEVER YOU WANT TO SAY IT, LEBRON HAS JAMMED A TON INTO JUST TWO SEASONS IN THE LEAGUE! BUT WE CAN'T FINISH UP LEBRON'S HIGHLIGHTS WITHOUT HIS RECORD-BREAKING 56-POINT GAME — NEXT!

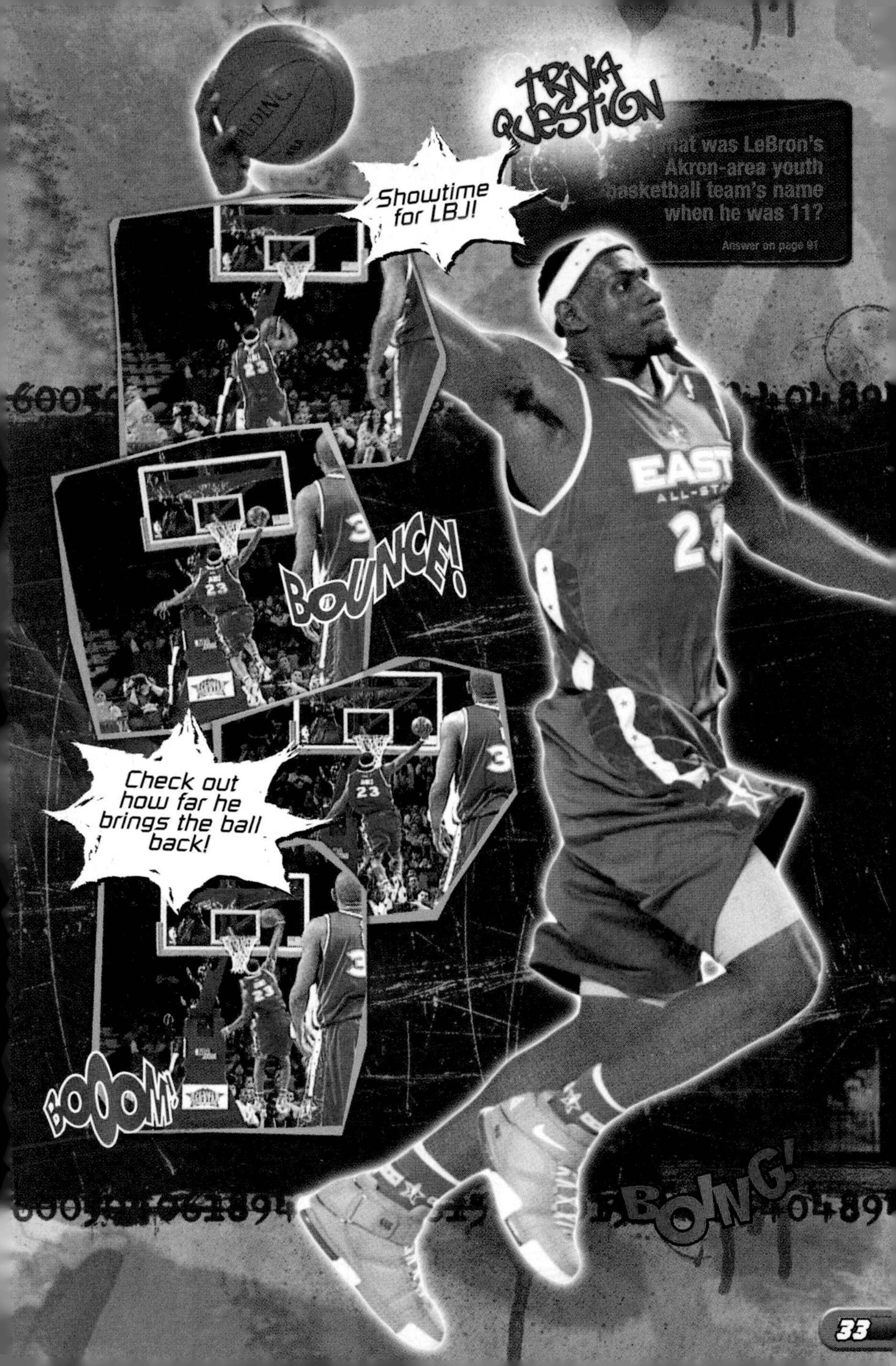
Showtime for LBJ!
BOUNCE!
Check out how far he brings the ball back!
BOOOM!
BOING!

TRIVIA QUESTION

What was LeBron's Akron-area youth basketball team's name when he was 11?

Answer on page 91

RECORD-BREAKING MOMENT!
56 POINTS!
3/20/05 vs. TORONTO!

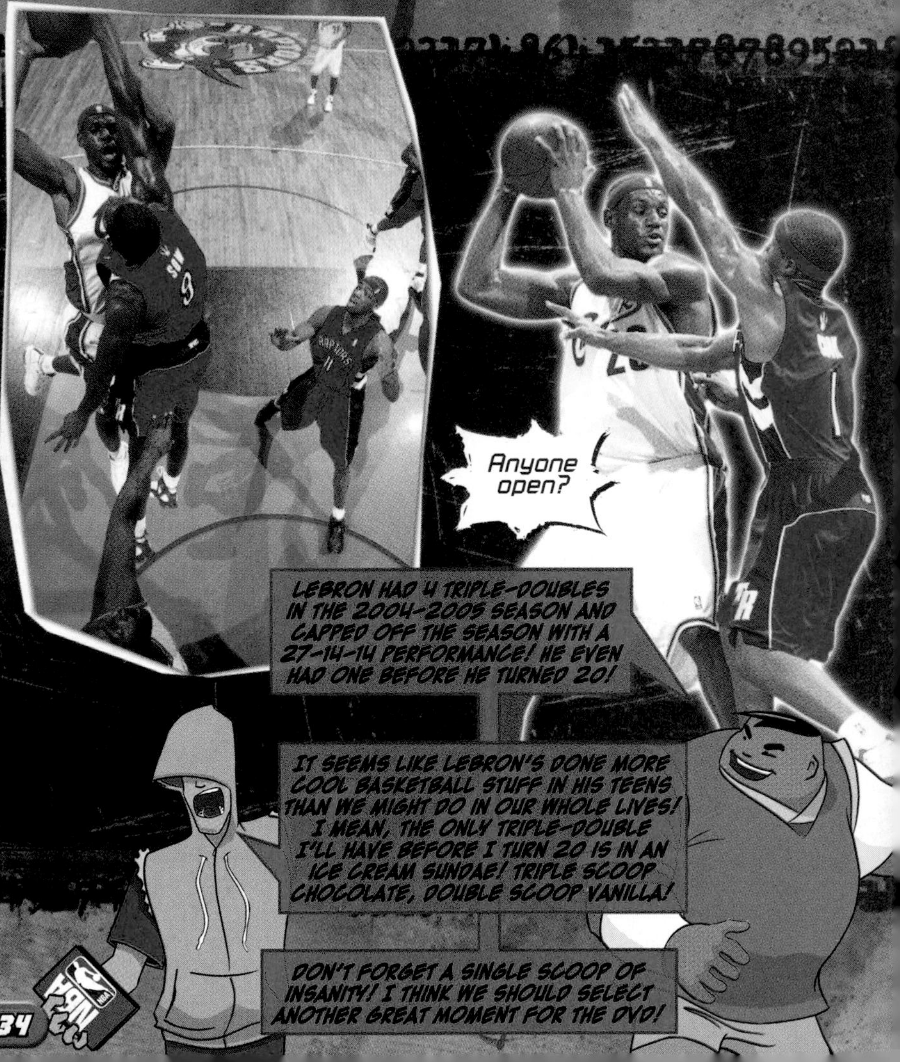

Anyone open?
LEBRON HAD 4 TRIPLE-DOUBLES IN THE 2004-2005 SEASON AND CAPPED OFF THE SEASON WITH A 27-14-14 PERFORMANCE! HE EVEN HAD ONE BEFORE HE TURNED 20!
IT SEEMS LIKE LEBRON'S DONE MORE COOL BASKETBALL STUFF IN HIS TEENS THAN WE MIGHT DO IN OUR WHOLE LIVES! I MEAN, THE ONLY TRIPLE-DOUBLE I'LL HAVE BEFORE I TURN 20 IS IN AN ICE CREAM SUNDAE! TRIPLE SCOOP CHOCOLATE, DOUBLE SCOOP VANILLA!
DON'T FORGET A SINGLE SCOOP OF INSANITY! I THINK WE SHOULD SELECT ANOTHER GREAT MOMENT FOR THE DVD!

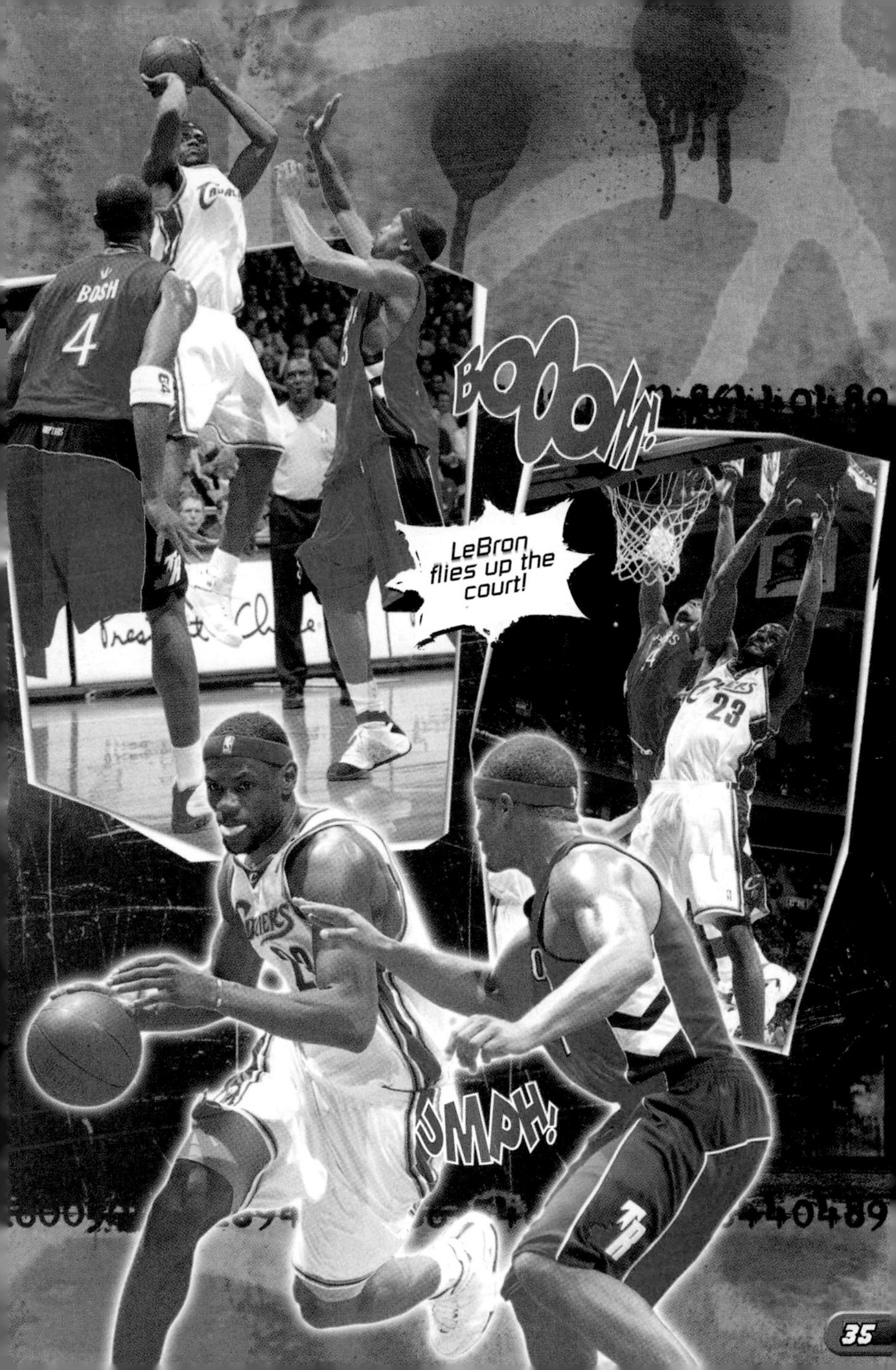
BOOOM!
LeBron flies up the court!
UMPH!

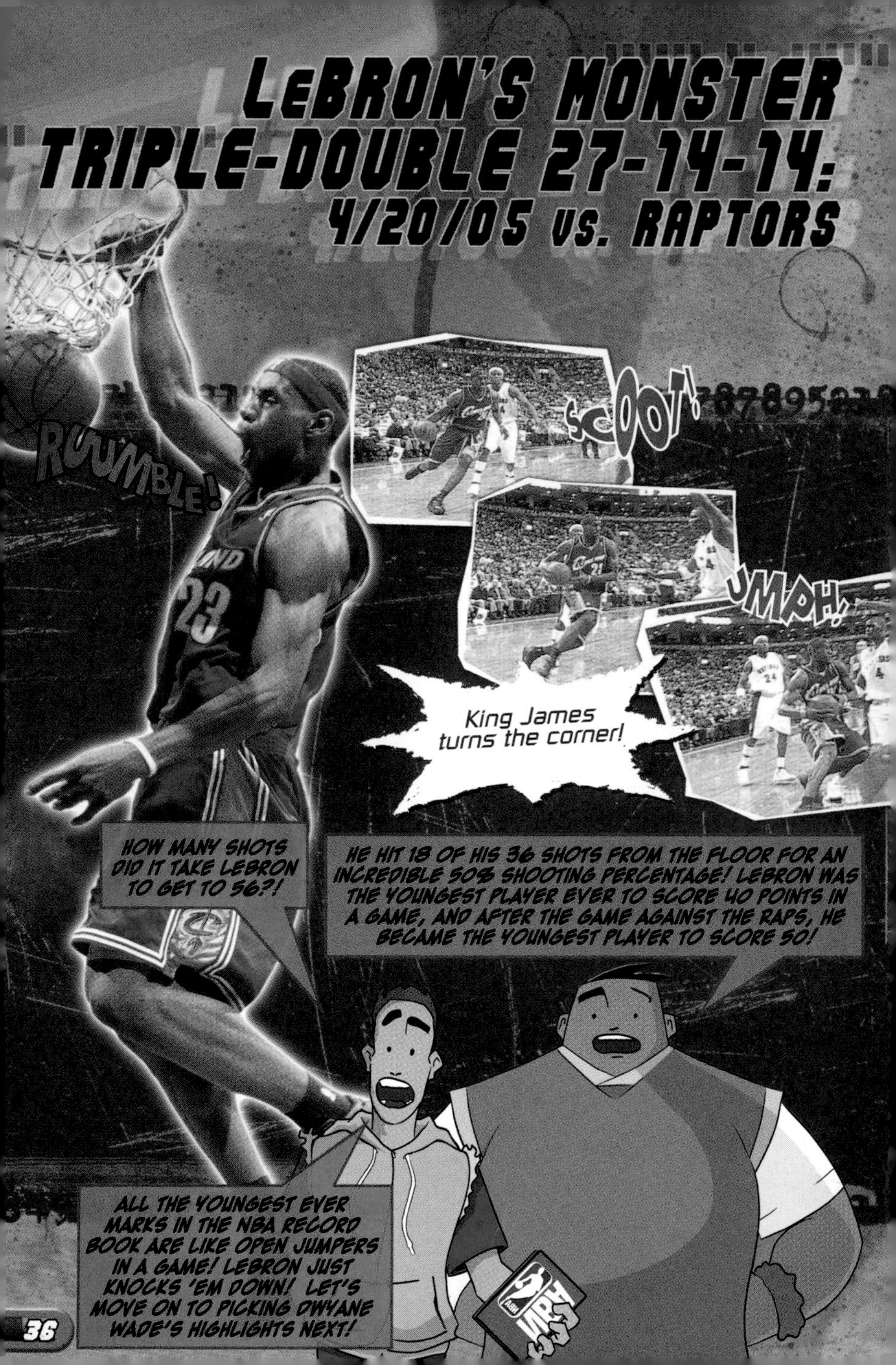
LeBRON'S MONSTER TRIPLE-DOUBLE 27-14-14:
4/20/05 vs. RAPTORS
RUUMBLE!
SCOOT!
UMPH!
King James turns the corner!
HOW MANY SHOTS DID IT TAKE LEBRON TO GET TO 56?!
HE HIT 18 OF HIS 36 SHOTS FROM THE FLOOR FOR AN INCREDIBLE 50% SHOOTING PERCENTAGE! LEBRON WAS THE YOUNGEST PLAYER EVER TO SCORE 40 POINTS IN A GAME, AND AFTER THE GAME AGAINST THE RAPS, HE BECAME THE YOUNGEST PLAYER TO SCORE 50!
ALL THE YOUNGEST EVER MARKS IN THE NBA RECORD BOOK ARE LIKE OPEN JUMPERS IN A GAME! LEBRON JUST KNOCKS 'EM DOWN! LET'S MOVE ON TO PICKING DWYANE WADE'S HIGHLIGHTS NEXT!

Trivia Question

What is the most number of minutes LeBron has played in a single game?

Answer on page 91

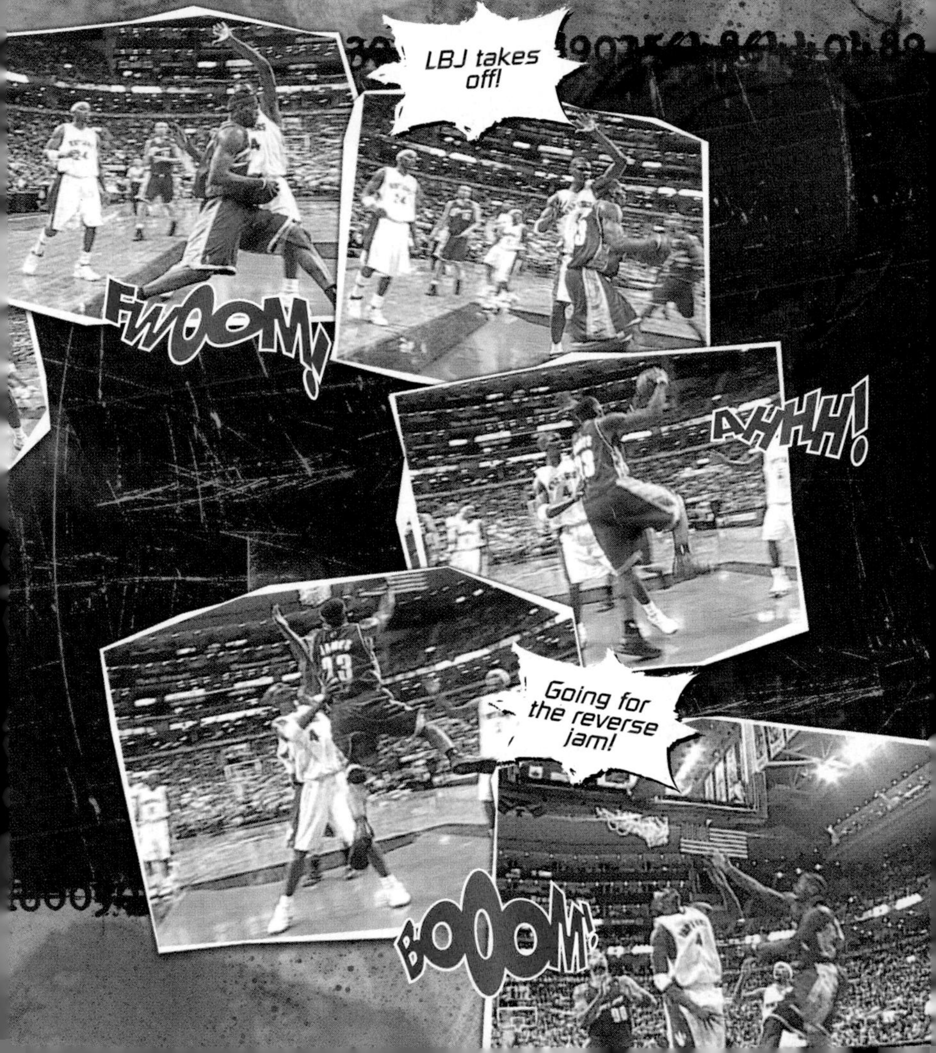

PLAYER SELECTED//:

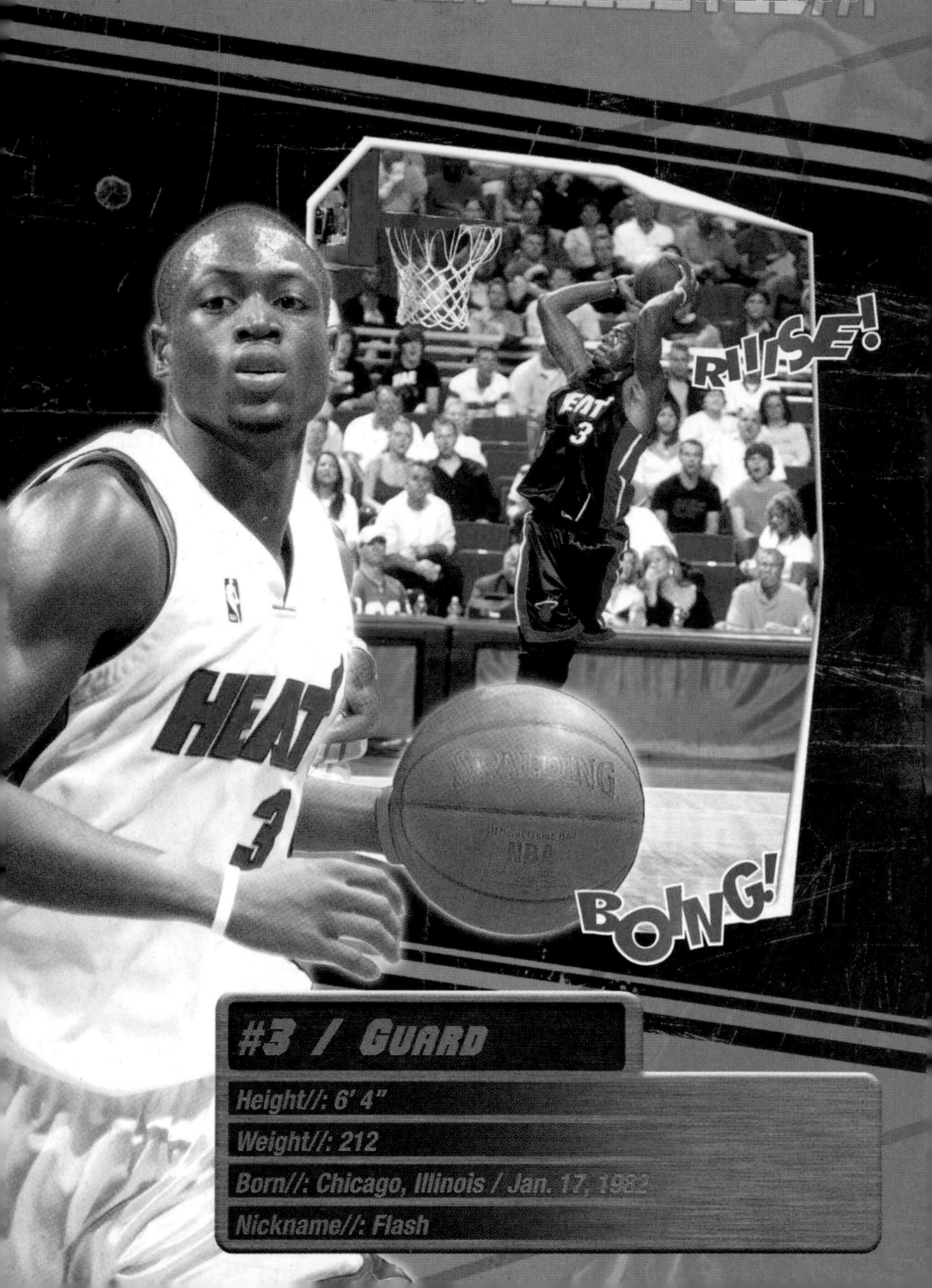
RISE!
HEAT
3
SPALDING
BOING!

#3 / GUARD

Height//: 6' 4"

Weight//: 212

Born//: Chicago, Illinois / Jan. 17, 1982

Nickname//: Flash

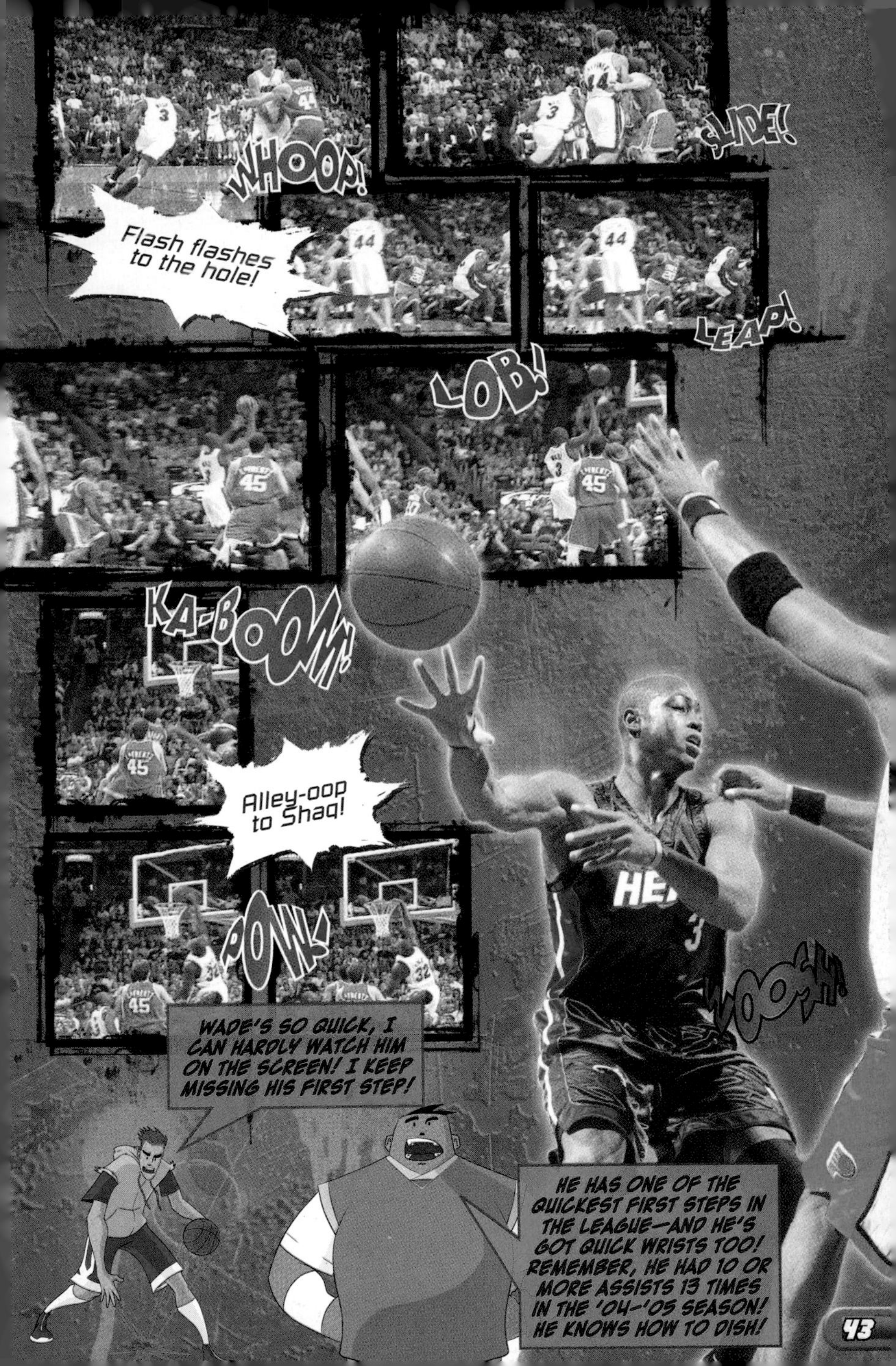
WHOOP!
SLIDE!
Flash flashes to the hole!
LEAP!
LOB!
KA-BOOM!
Alley-oop to Shaq!
POW!
WOOSH!
WADE'S SO QUICK, I CAN HARDLY WATCH HIM ON THE SCREEN! I KEEP MISSING HIS FIRST STEP!
HE HAS ONE OF THE QUICKEST FIRST STEPS IN THE LEAGUE—AND HE'S GOT QUICK WRISTS TOO! REMEMBER, HE HAD 10 OR MORE ASSISTS 13 TIMES IN THE '04-'05 SEASON! HE KNOWS HOW TO DISH!

GREAT MOMENT UNLOCKED!

39-POINT GAME!

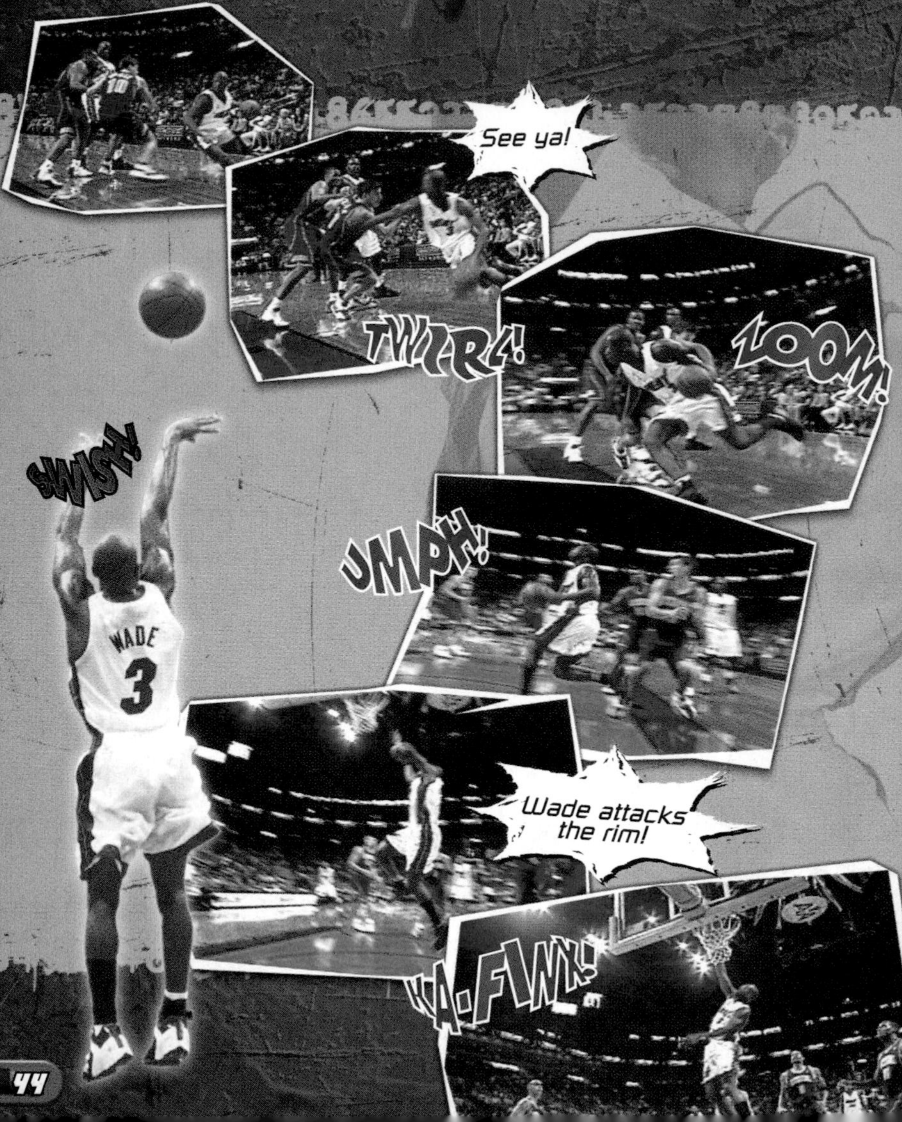
See ya!
TWIRL!
ZOOM!
SWISH!
WADE
3
UMPH!
Wade attacks the rim!
KA-FLINK!

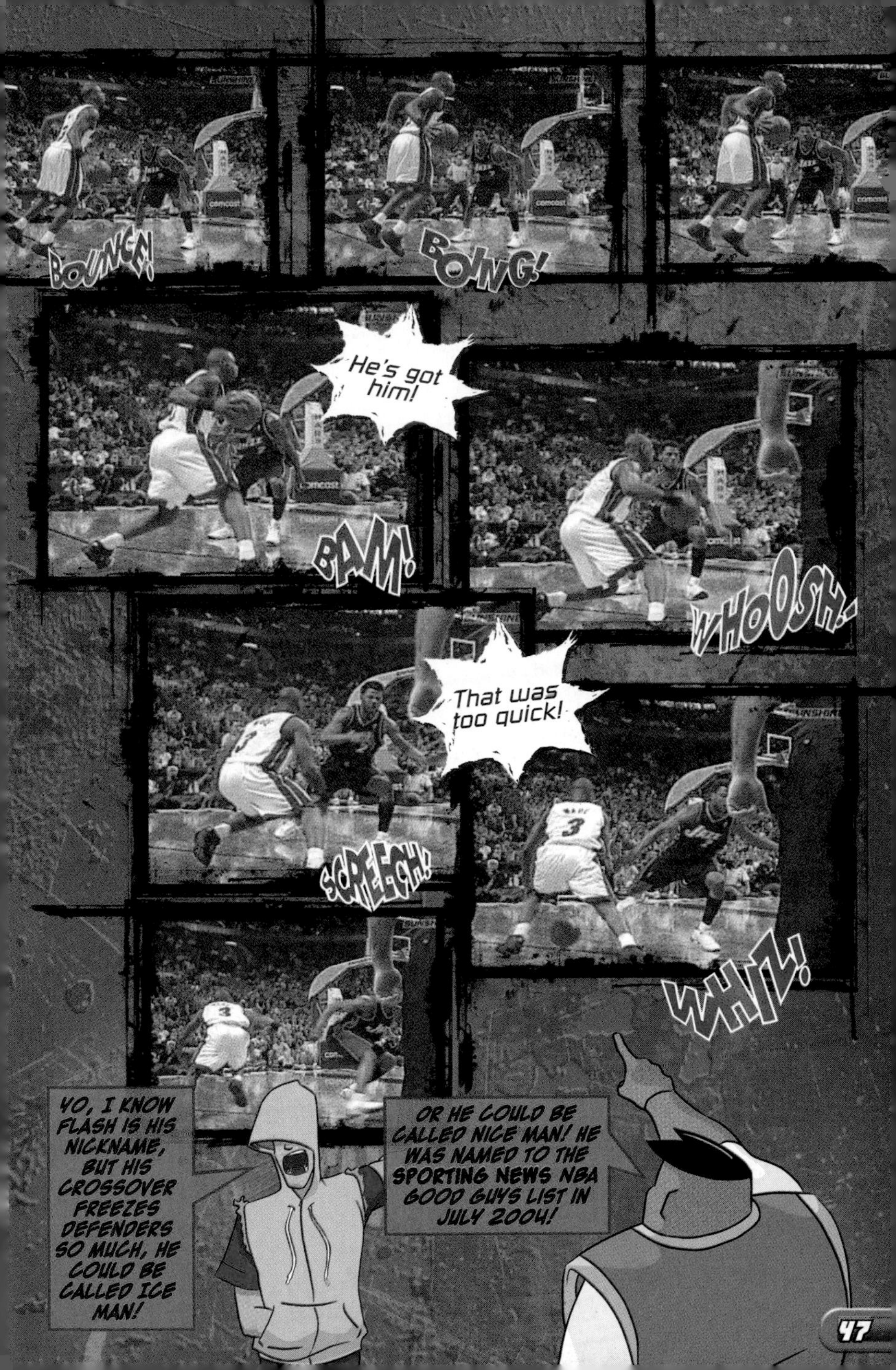
BOUNCE!
BOING!
He's got him!
BAM!
WHOOSH!
That was too quick!
SCREECH!
WHIZ!
YO, I KNOW FLASH IS HIS NICKNAME, BUT HIS CROSSOVER FREEZES DEFENDERS SO MUCH, HE COULD BE CALLED ICE MAN!
OR HE COULD BE CALLED NICE MAN! HE WAS NAMED TO THE SPORTING NEWS NBA GOOD GUYS LIST IN JULY 2004!

SKILL #4//:
- UNBELIEVABLE DUNK!

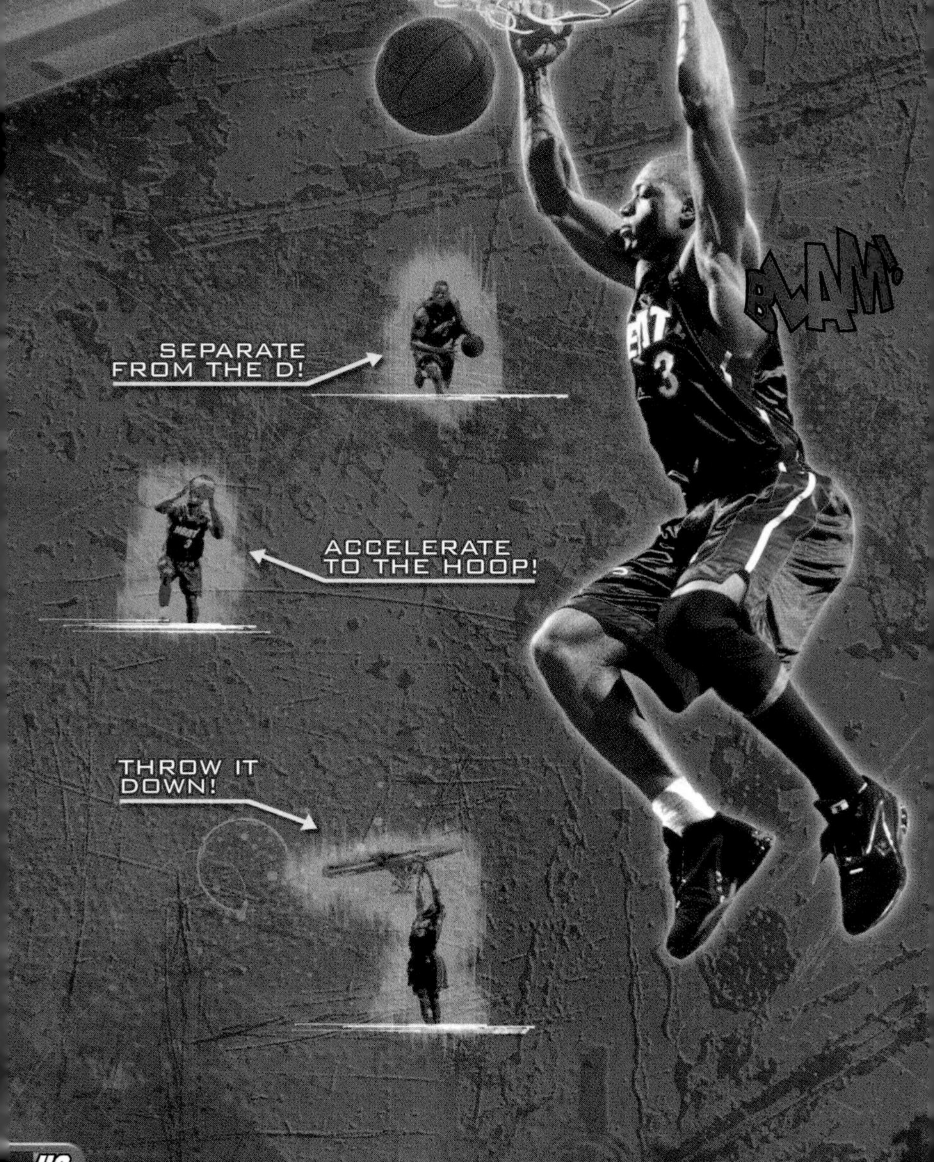
BLAM!
SEPARATE FROM THE D!
ACCELERATE TO THE HOOP!
THROW IT DOWN!

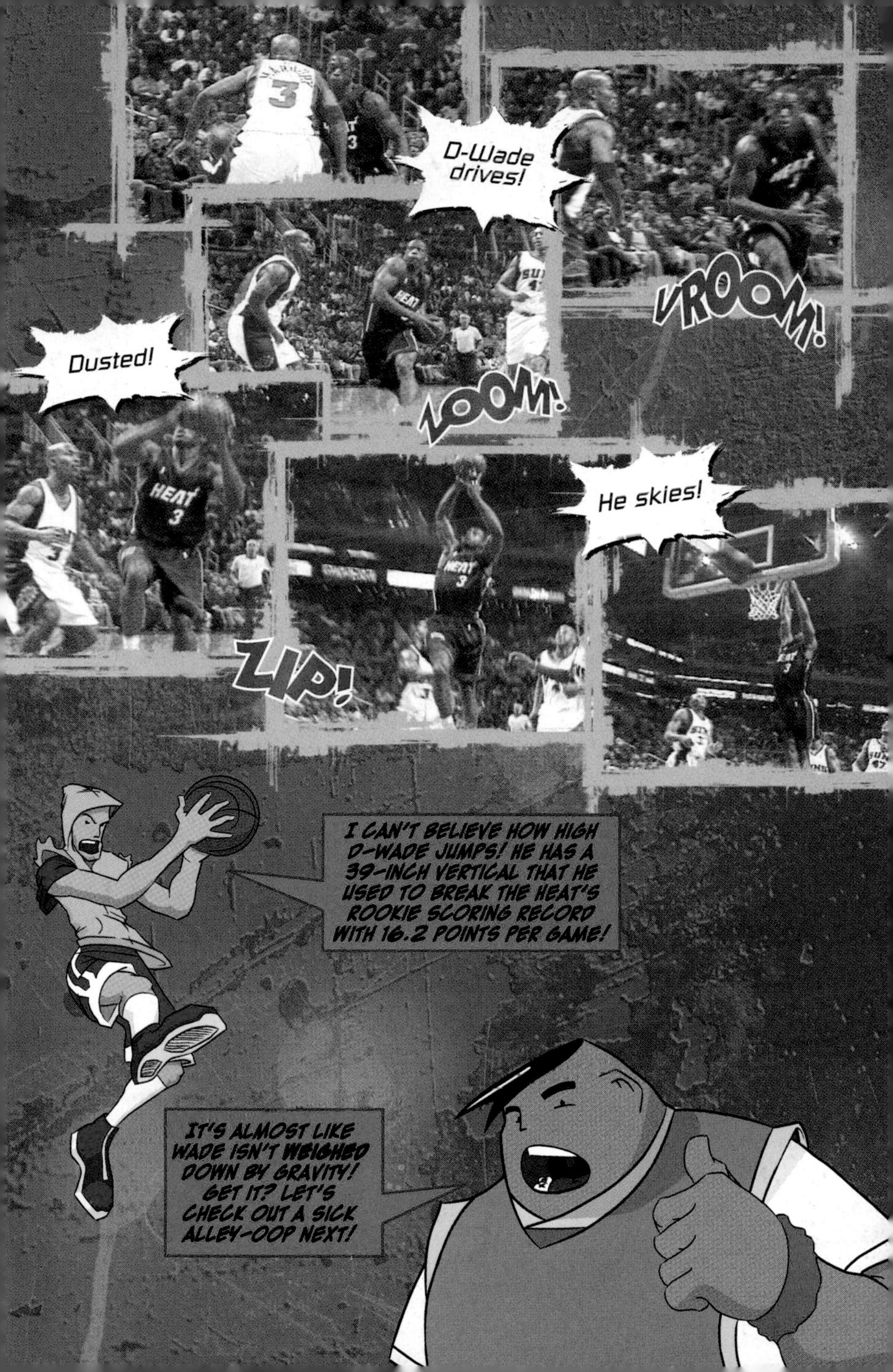
D-Wade drives!
VROOM!
Dusted!
ZOOM!
He skies!
ZIP!
I CAN'T BELIEVE HOW HIGH D-WADE JUMPS! HE HAS A 39-INCH VERTICAL THAT HE USED TO BREAK THE HEAT'S ROOKIE SCORING RECORD WITH 16.2 POINTS PER GAME!
IT'S ALMOST LIKE WADE ISN'T WEIGHED DOWN BY GRAVITY! GET IT? LET'S CHECK OUT A SICK ALLEY-OOP NEXT!

SKILL #5//: - ALLEY OOP!

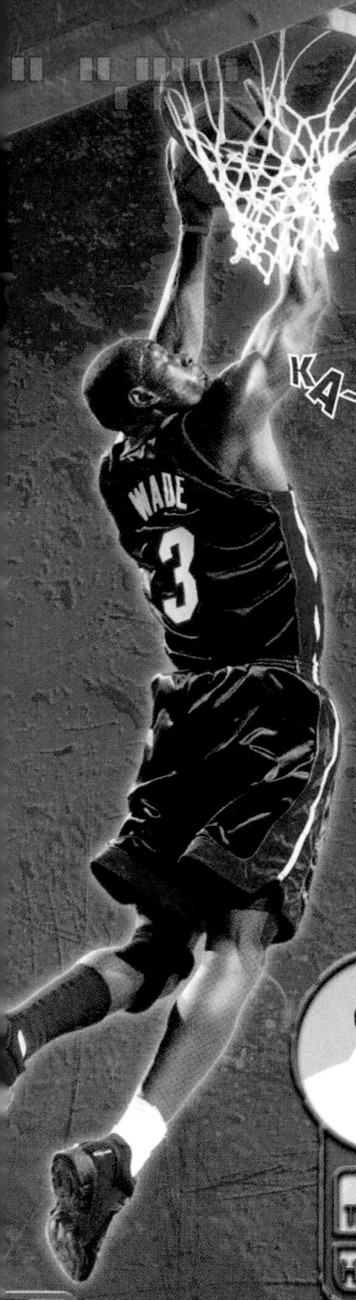
WADE
3
KA-SLAAM!

EYE UP THE BALL!

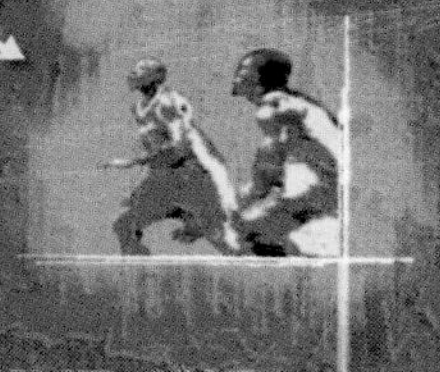

JUMP AND CATCH!

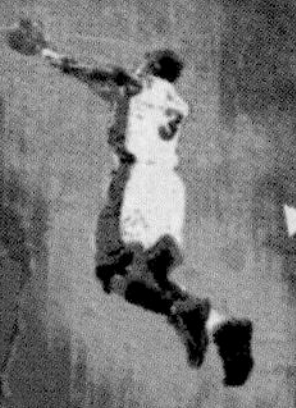

FINISH STRONG WITH THE DUNK!

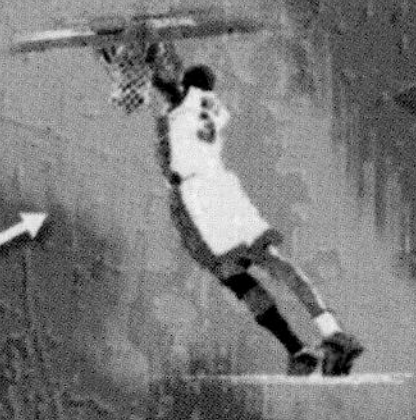

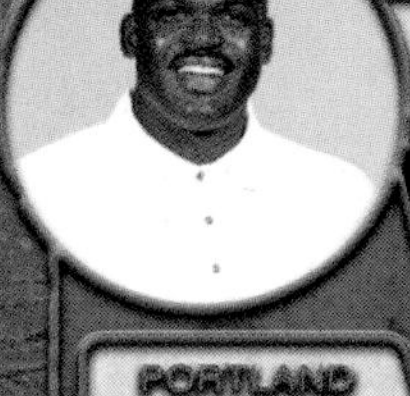

NATE McMILLAN

PORTLAND TRAILBLAZERS

HEAD COACH

"He does a really good job of splitting the defense and getting to the basket."[6]

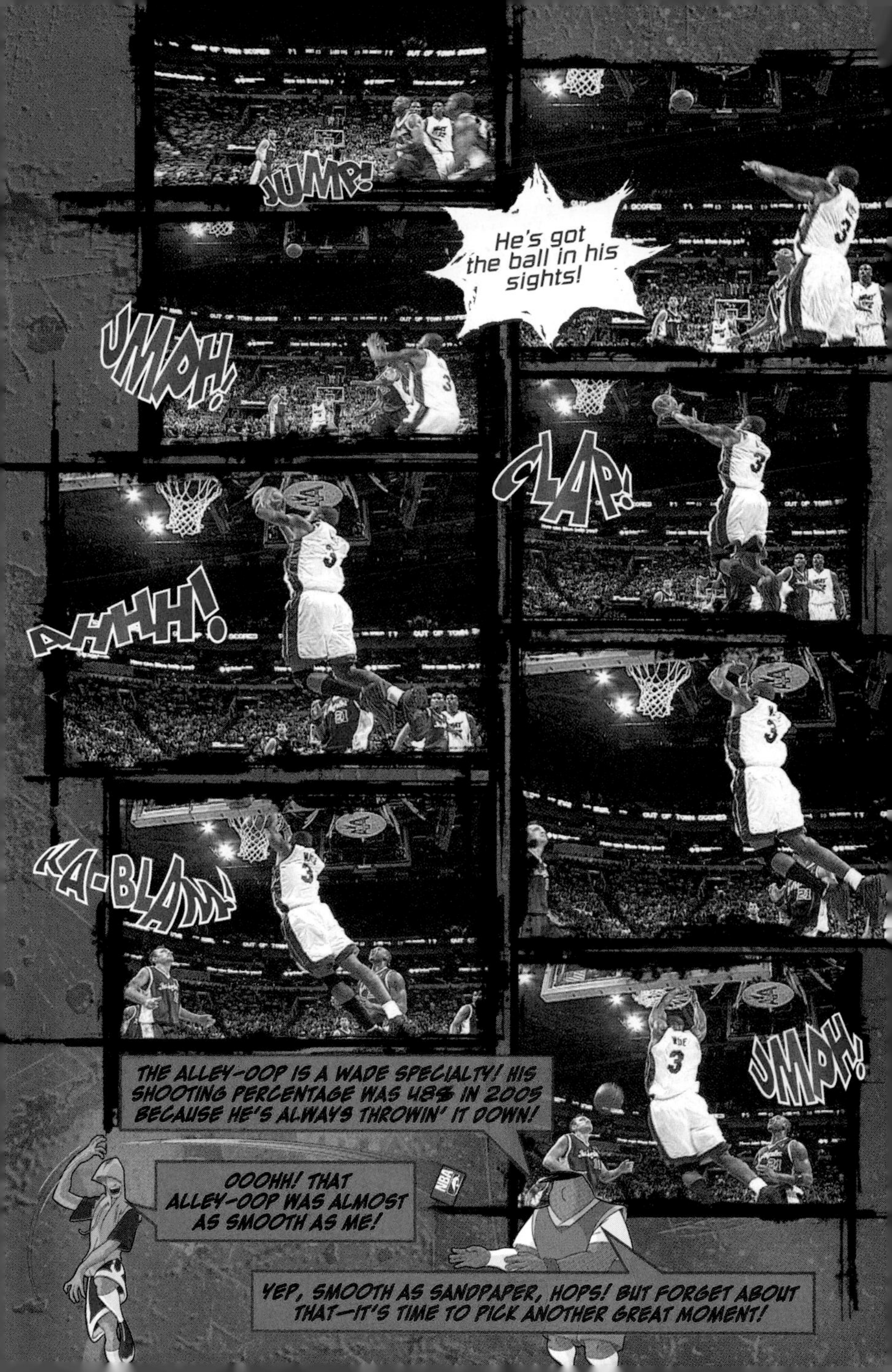
JUMP!
He's got the ball in his sights!
UMPH!
CLAP!
AHHH!
KA-BLAM!
UMPH!
THE ALLEY-OOP IS A WADE SPECIALTY! HIS SHOOTING PERCENTAGE WAS 48% IN 2005 BECAUSE HE'S ALWAYS THROWIN' IT DOWN!
OOOHH! THAT ALLEY-OOP WAS ALMOST AS SMOOTH AS ME!
YEP, SMOOTH AS SANDPAPER, HOPS! BUT FORGET ABOUT THAT—IT'S TIME TO PICK ANOTHER GREAT MOMENT!

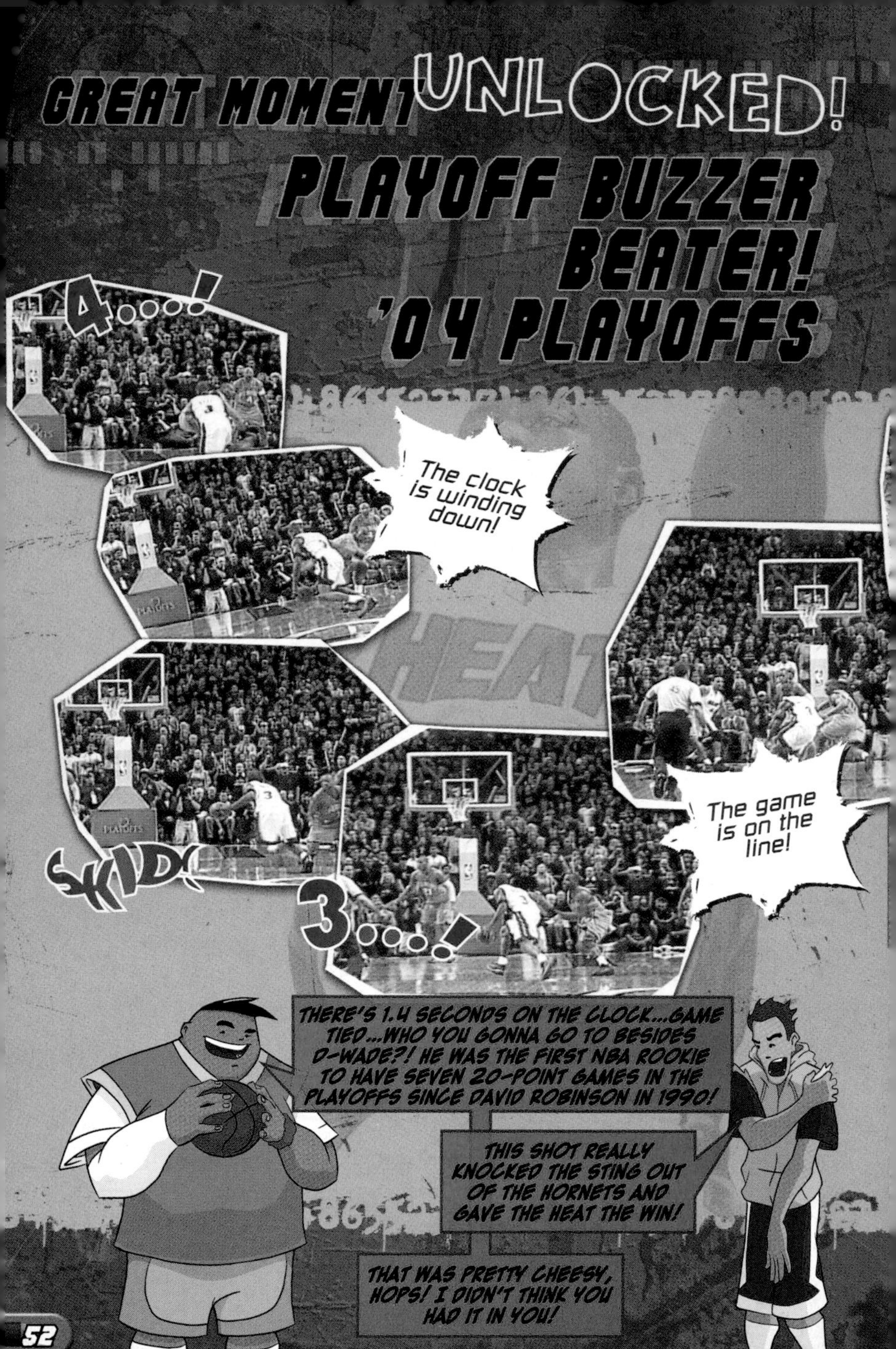
GREAT MOMENT UNLOCKED!
PLAYOFF BUZZER BEATER! '04 PLAYOFFS
4...!
The clock is winding down!
SKID!
3...!
The game is on the line!
THERE'S 1.4 SECONDS ON THE CLOCK...GAME TIED...WHO YOU GONNA GO TO BESIDES D-WADE?! HE WAS THE FIRST NBA ROOKIE TO HAVE SEVEN 20-POINT GAMES IN THE PLAYOFFS SINCE DAVID ROBINSON IN 1990!
THIS SHOT REALLY KNOCKED THE STING OUT OF THE HORNETS AND GAVE THE HEAT THE WIN!
THAT WAS PRETTY CHEESY, HOPS! I DIDN'T THINK YOU HAD IT IN YOU!

TRIVIA QUESTION

What are Dwyane's two favorite foods?

Answer on page 91

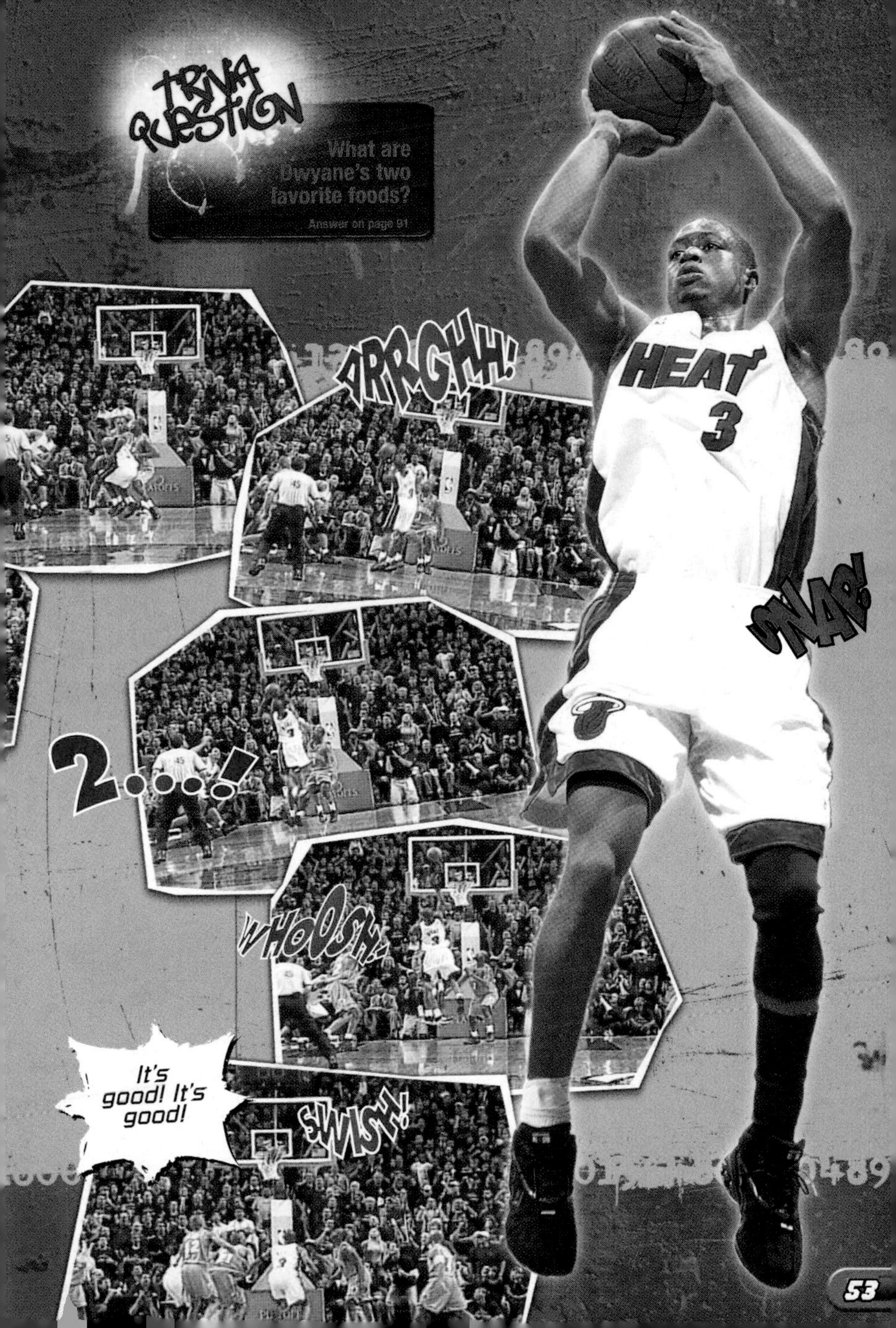
ARRGHH!
SNAP!
2....!
WHOOSH!
It's good! It's good!
SWISH!

SKILL #6//:

- HALF-COURT ALLEY-OOP!

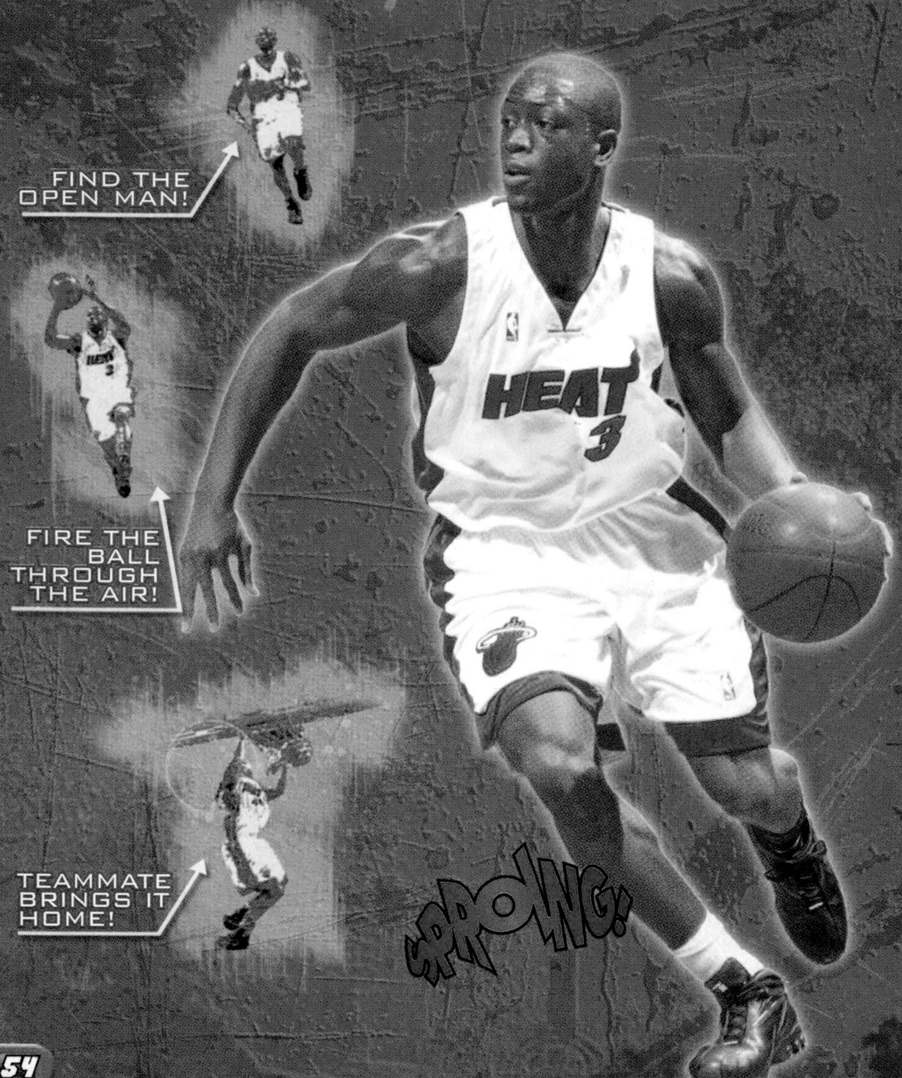
FIND THE OPEN MAN!
FIRE THE BALL THROUGH THE AIR!
TEAMMATE BRINGS IT HOME!
HEAT
3
SPROING!

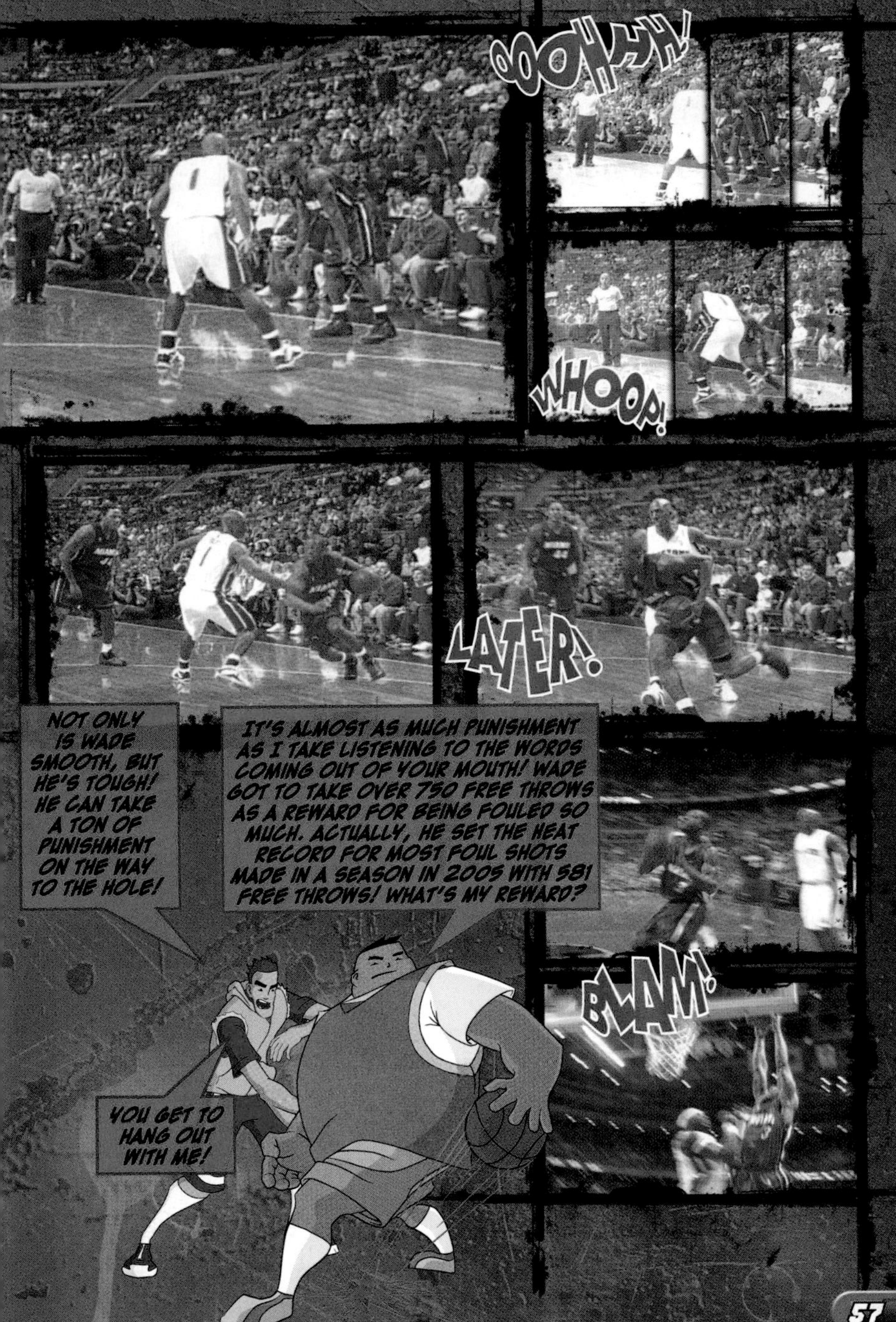
OOHHH!
WHOOP!
LATER!
NOT ONLY IS WADE SMOOTH, BUT HE'S TOUGH! HE CAN TAKE A TON OF PUNISHMENT ON THE WAY TO THE HOLE!
IT'S ALMOST AS MUCH PUNISHMENT AS I TAKE LISTENING TO THE WORDS COMING OUT OF YOUR MOUTH! WADE GOT TO TAKE OVER 750 FREE THROWS AS A REWARD FOR BEING FOULED SO MUCH. ACTUALLY, HE SET THE HEAT RECORD FOR MOST FOUL SHOTS MADE IN A SEASON IN 2005 WITH 581 FREE THROWS! WHAT'S MY REWARD?
YOU GET TO HANG OUT WITH ME!
BLAM!

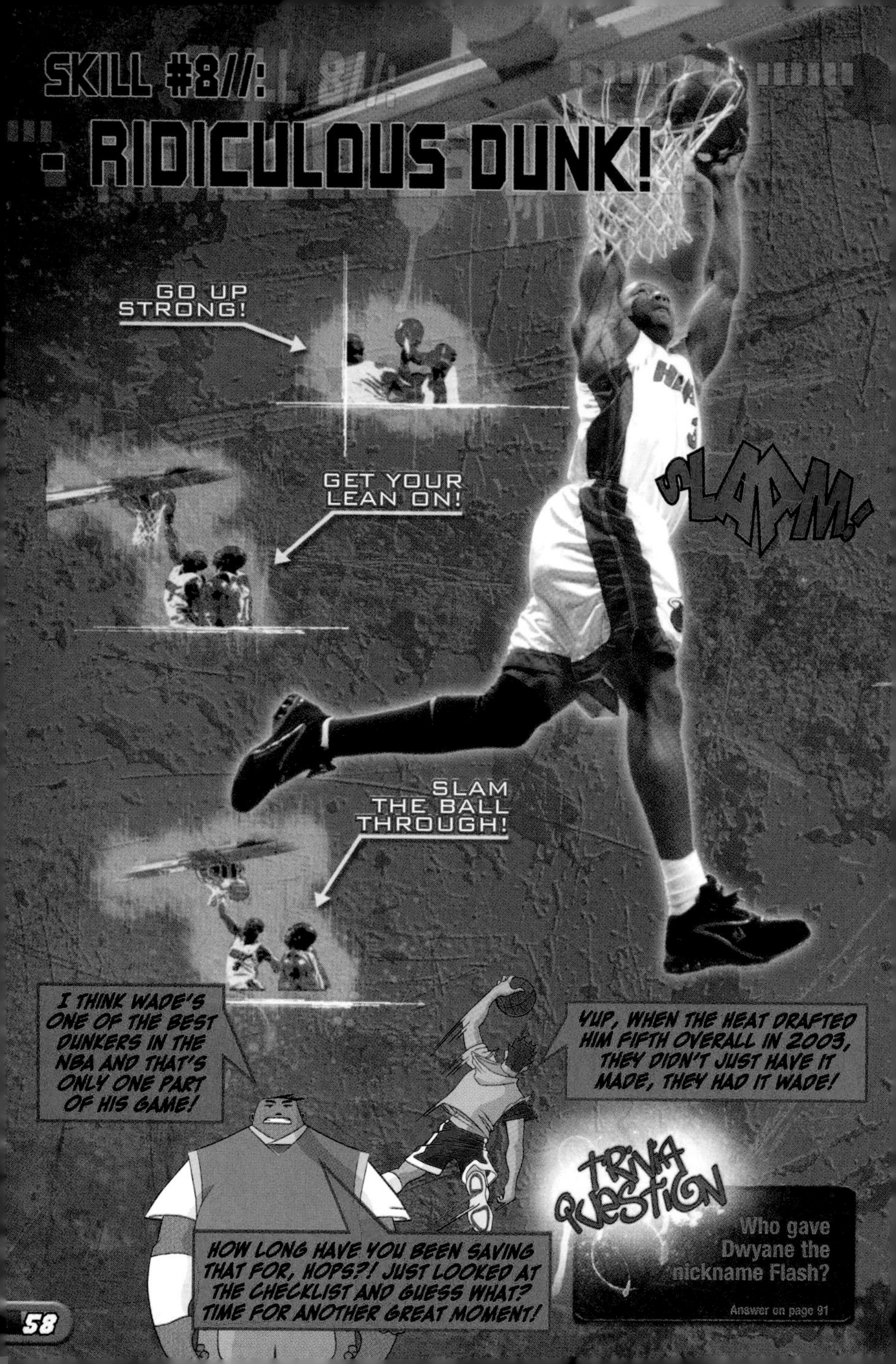

SKILL #8//:
- RIDICULOUS DUNK!
GO UP STRONG!
GET YOUR LEAN ON!
SLAM THE BALL THROUGH!
SLAM!
I THINK WADE'S ONE OF THE BEST DUNKERS IN THE NBA AND THAT'S ONLY ONE PART OF HIS GAME!
YUP, WHEN THE HEAT DRAFTED HIM FIFTH OVERALL IN 2003, THEY DIDN'T JUST HAVE IT MADE, THEY HAD IT WADE!
HOW LONG HAVE YOU BEEN SAVING THAT FOR, HOPS?! JUST LOOKED AT THE CHECKLIST AND GUESS WHAT? TIME FOR ANOTHER GREAT MOMENT!
TRIVIA QUESTION
Who gave Dwyane the nickname Flash?
Answer on page 91

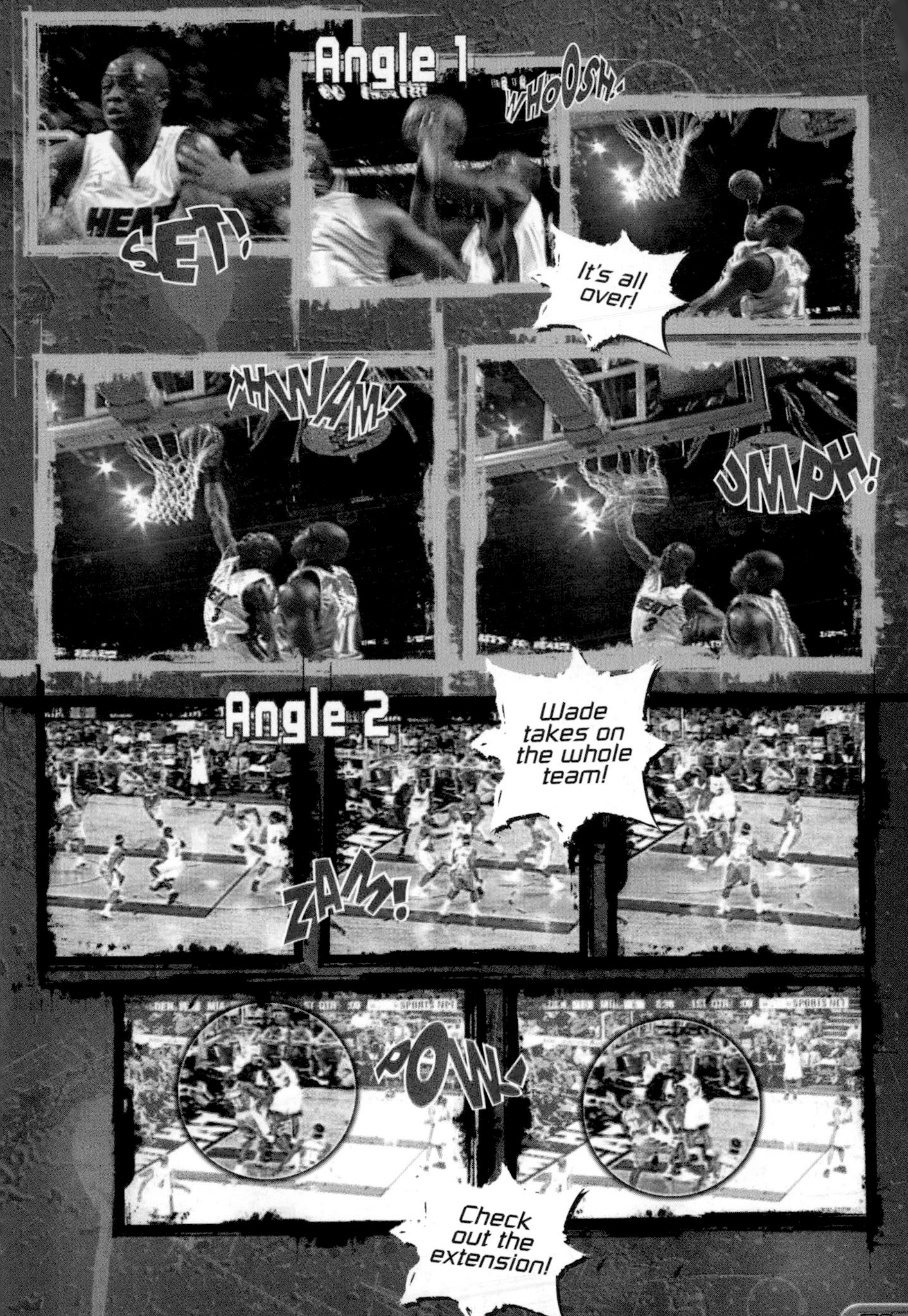
Angle 1
SET!
WHOOSH!
It's all over!
THWAM!
UMPH!
Angle 2
Wade takes on the whole team!
ZAM!
POW!
Check out the extension!

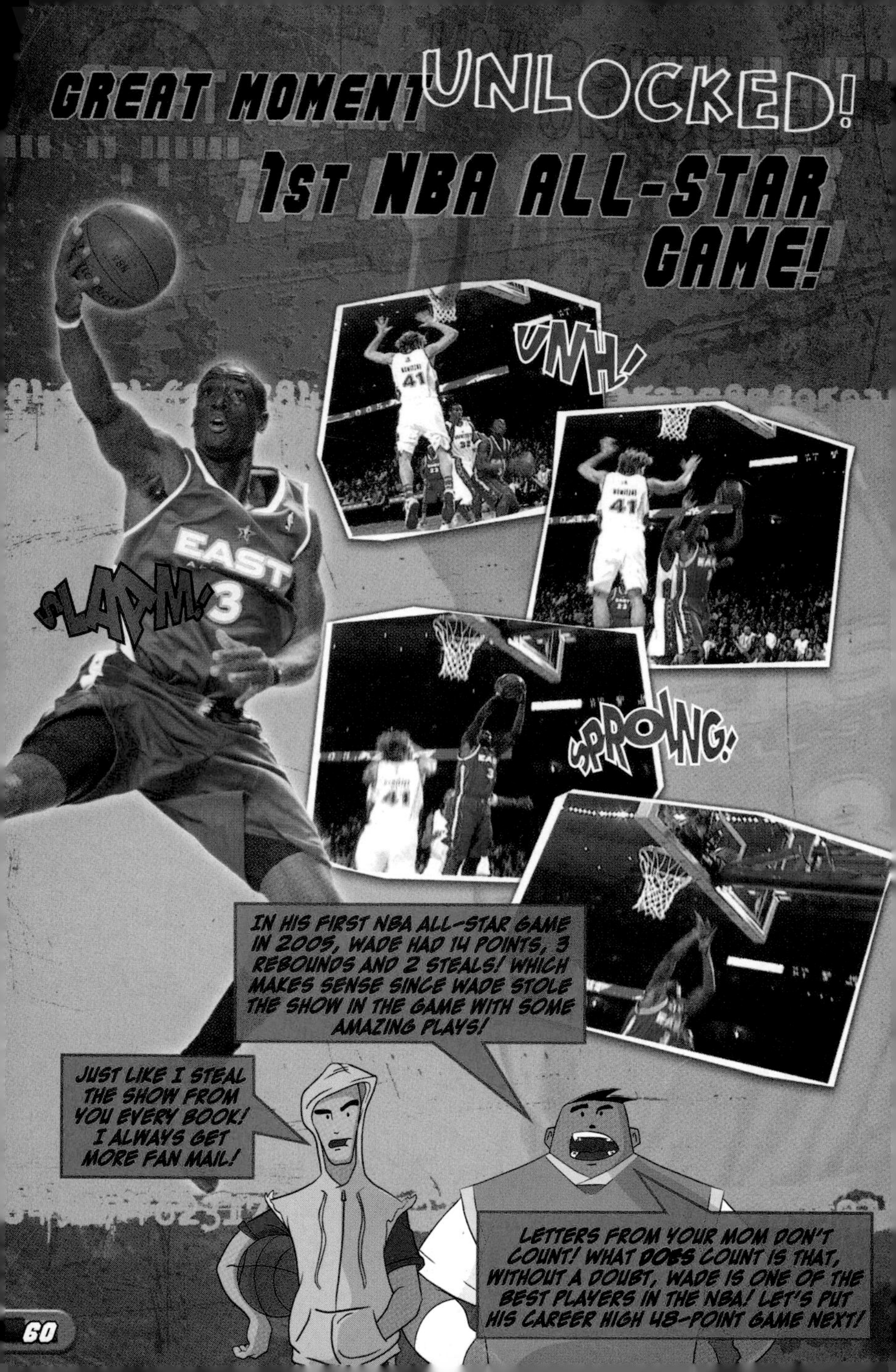
GREAT MOMENT UNLOCKED!
1ST NBA ALL-STAR GAME!
UNH!
SLAM!
SPROING!
IN HIS FIRST NBA ALL-STAR GAME IN 2005, WADE HAD 14 POINTS, 3 REBOUNDS AND 2 STEALS! WHICH MAKES SENSE SINCE WADE STOLE THE SHOW IN THE GAME WITH SOME AMAZING PLAYS!
JUST LIKE I STEAL THE SHOW FROM YOU EVERY BOOK! I ALWAYS GET MORE FAN MAIL!
LETTERS FROM YOUR MOM DON'T COUNT! WHAT DOES COUNT IS THAT, WITHOUT A DOUBT, WADE IS ONE OF THE BEST PLAYERS IN THE NBA! LET'S PUT HIS CAREER HIGH 48-POINT GAME NEXT!

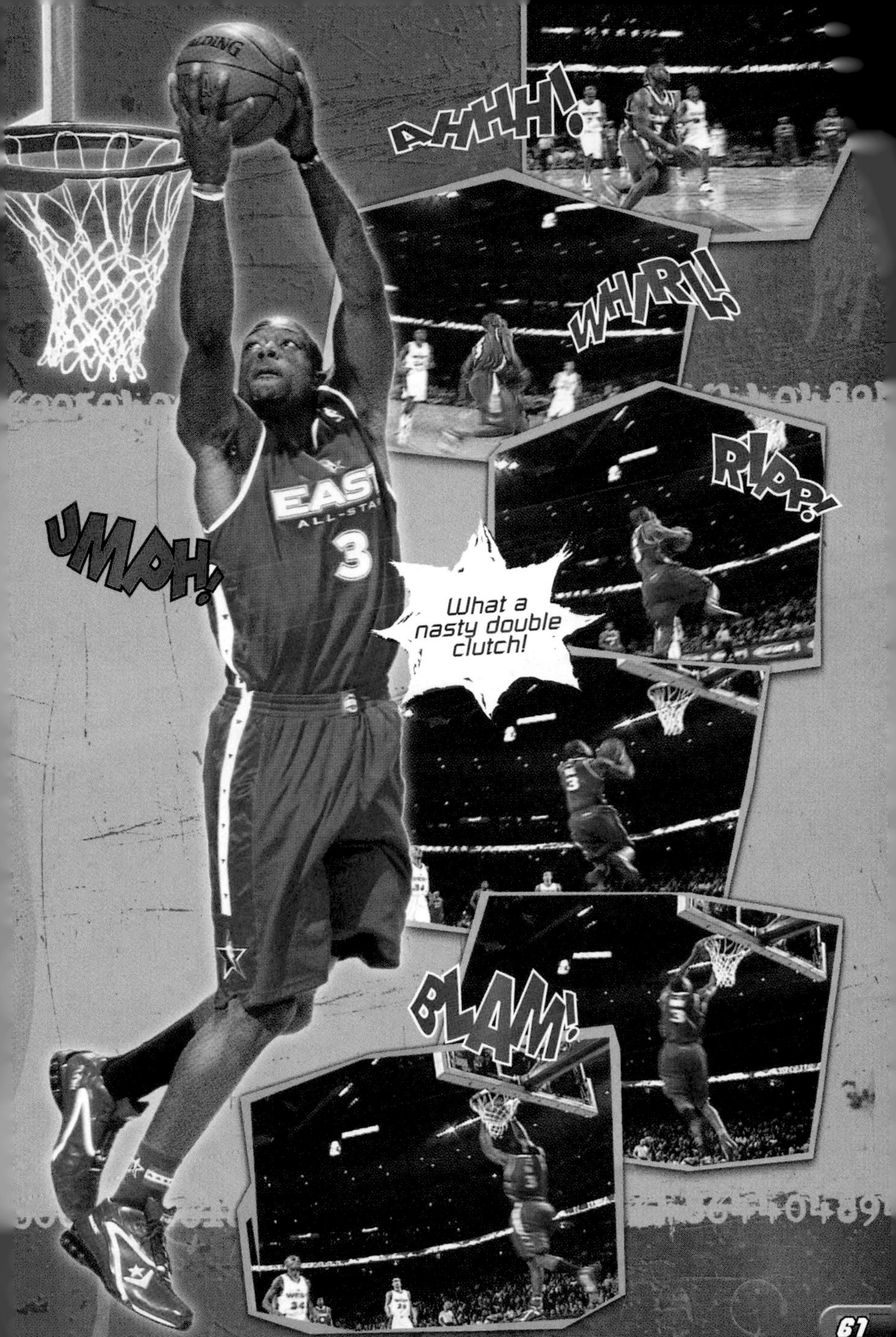
AHHH!
WHIRL!
RIPP!
UMOH!
What a nasty double clutch!
BLAM!

CAREER HIGH 48-POINT GAME! 4/14/05 vs. PHILLY

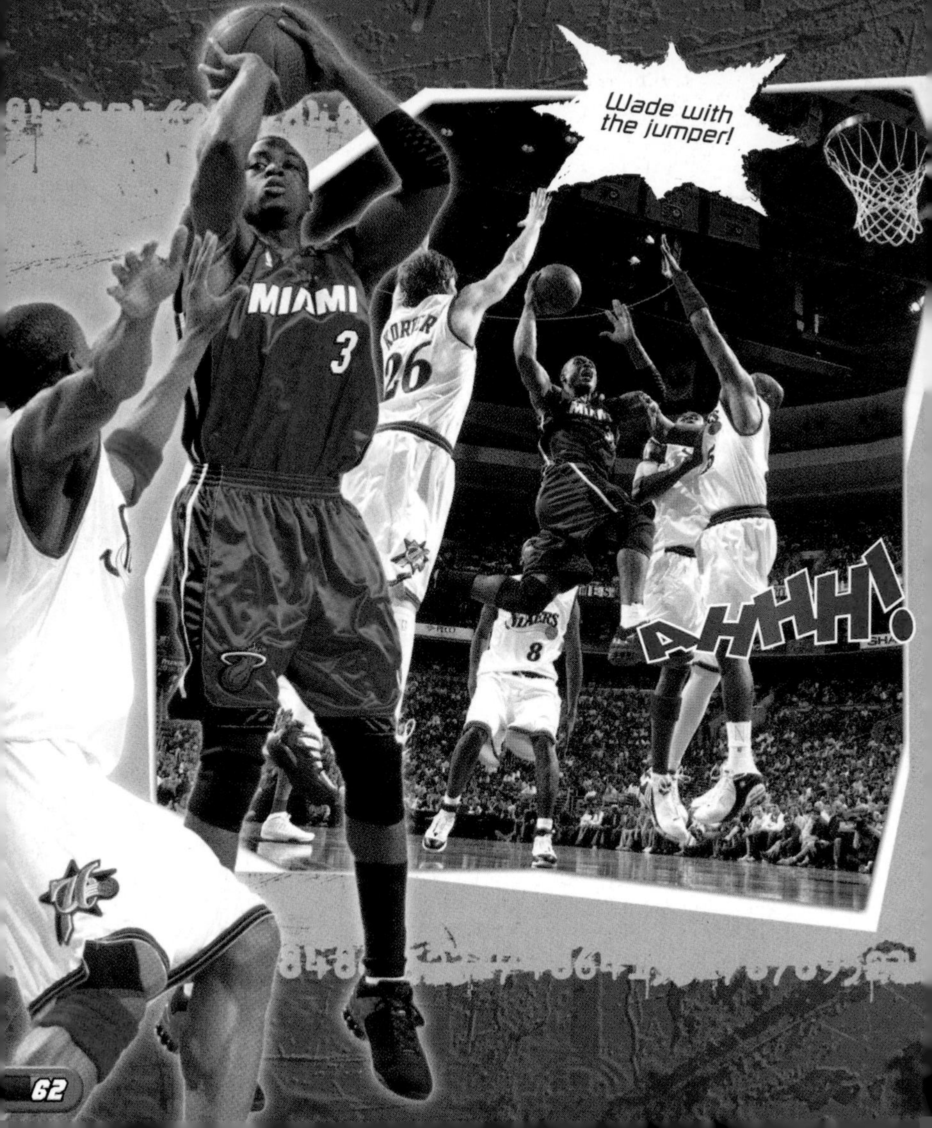
Wade with the jumper!
AHHHH!

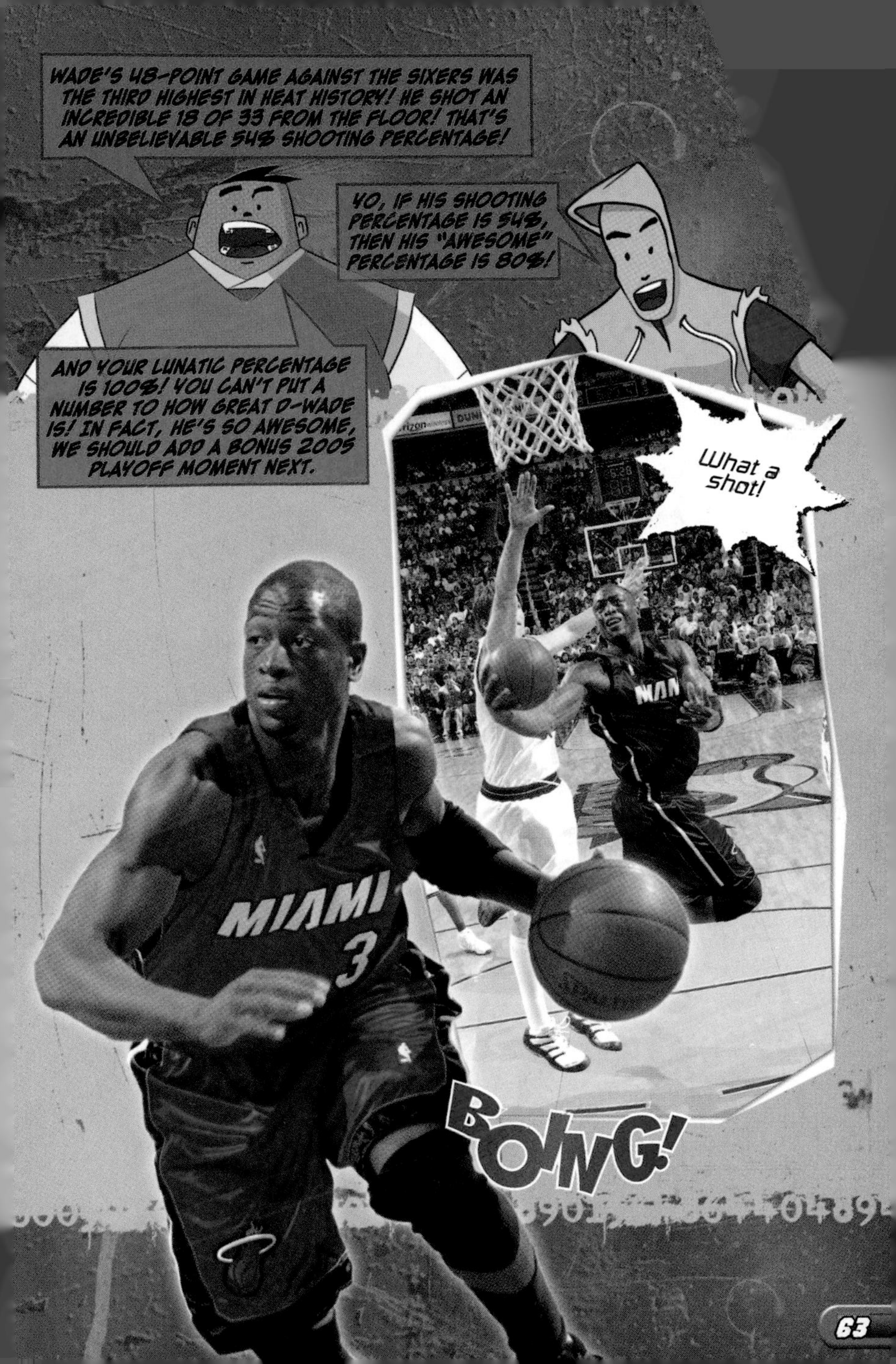
WADE'S 48-POINT GAME AGAINST THE SIXERS WAS THE THIRD HIGHEST IN HEAT HISTORY! HE SHOT AN INCREDIBLE 18 OF 33 FROM THE FLOOR! THAT'S AN UNBELIEVABLE 54% SHOOTING PERCENTAGE!
YO, IF HIS SHOOTING PERCENTAGE IS 54%, THEN HIS "AWESOME" PERCENTAGE IS 80%!
AND YOUR LUNATIC PERCENTAGE IS 100%! YOU CAN'T PUT A NUMBER TO HOW GREAT D-WADE IS! IN FACT, HE'S SO AWESOME, WE SHOULD ADD A BONUS 2005 PLAYOFF MOMENT NEXT.
What a shot!
MIAMI
3
BOING!

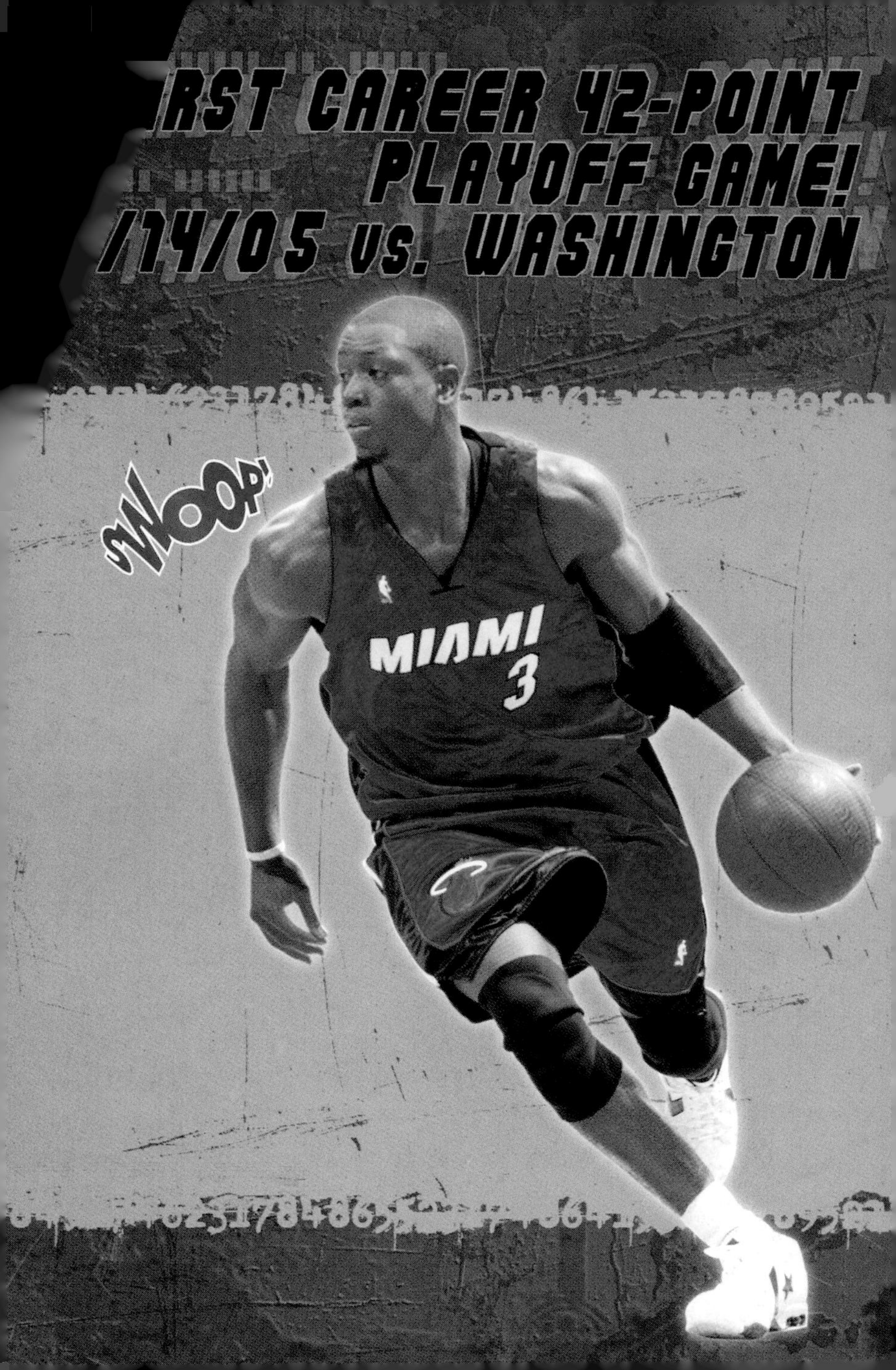
RST CAREER 42-POINT
PLAYOFF GAME!
/14/05 vs. WASHINGTON
MIAMI
3

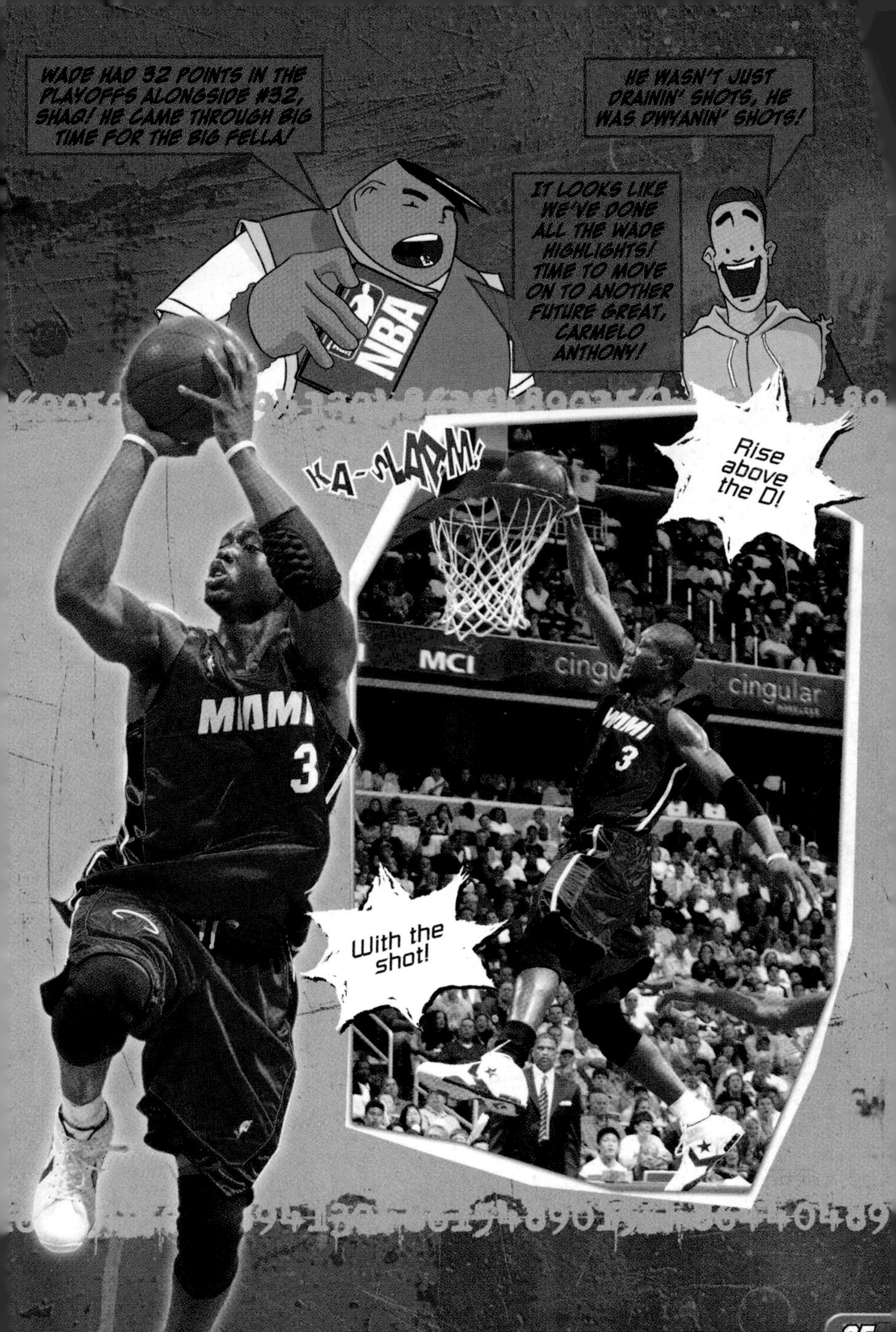
WADE HAD 32 POINTS IN THE PLAYOFFS ALONGSIDE #32, SHAQ! HE CAME THROUGH BIG TIME FOR THE BIG FELLA!
HE WASN'T JUST DRAININ' SHOTS, HE WAS DWYANIN' SHOTS!
IT LOOKS LIKE WE'VE DONE ALL THE WADE HIGHLIGHTS! TIME TO MOVE ON TO ANOTHER FUTURE GREAT, CARMELO ANTHONY!
KA-SLAM!
Rise above the D!
With the shot!

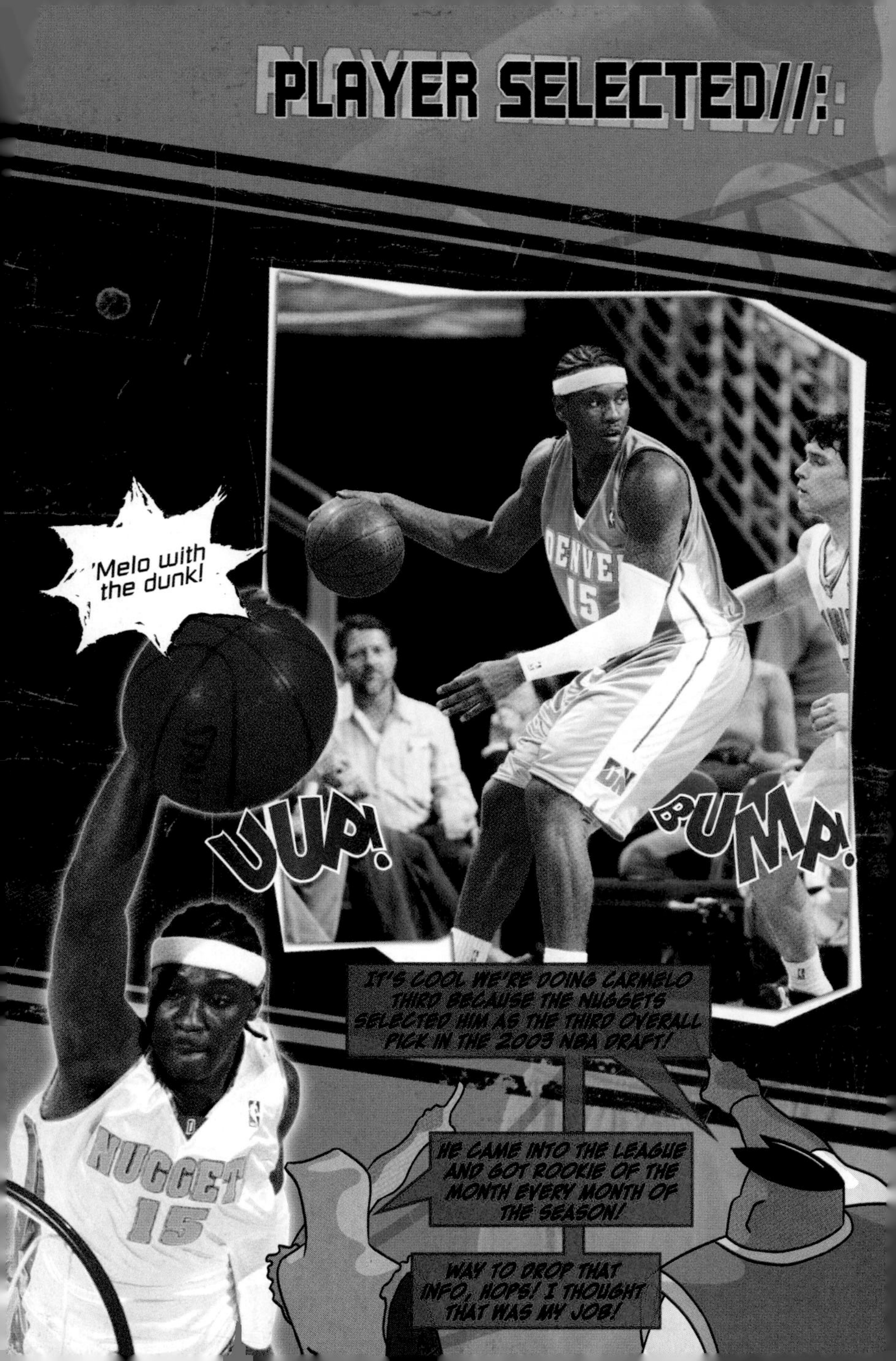
PLAYER SELECTED//:
'Melo with the dunk!
UUP!
BUMP!
IT'S COOL WE'RE DOING CARMELO THIRD BECAUSE THE NUGGETS SELECTED HIM AS THE THIRD OVERALL PICK IN THE 2003 NBA DRAFT!
HE CAME INTO THE LEAGUE AND GOT ROOKIE OF THE MONTH EVERY MONTH OF THE SEASON!
WAY TO DROP THAT INFO, HOPS! I THOUGHT THAT WAS MY JOB!

Angle 1

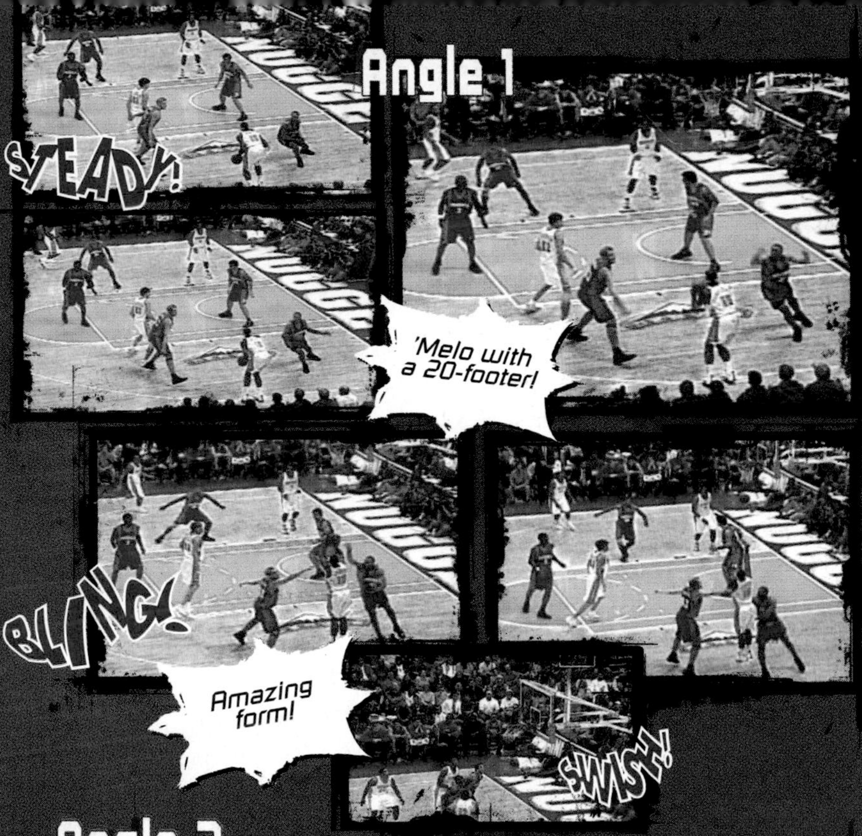
STEADY!
'Melo with a 20-footer!
BLING!
Amazing form!
SWISH!

Angle 2

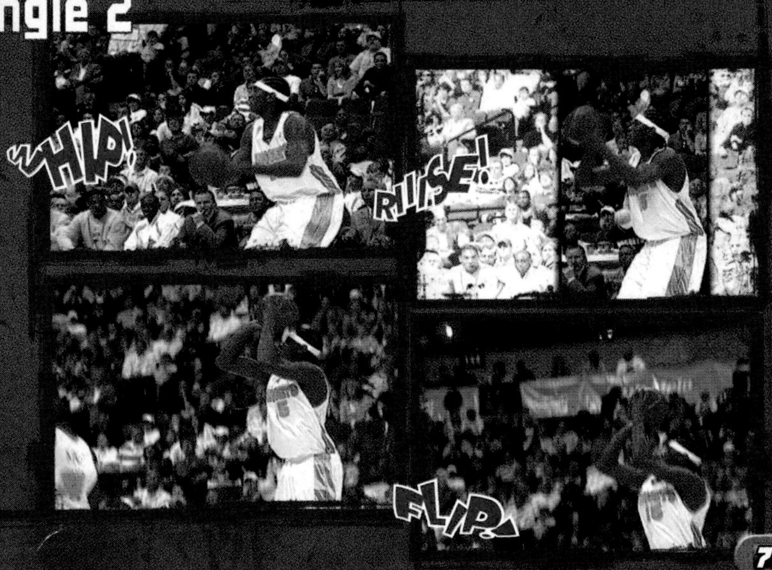
WHIP!
RIIISE!
FLIP!

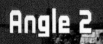

GREAT MOMENT UNLOCKED!

2ND YOUNGEST TO SCORE 40!

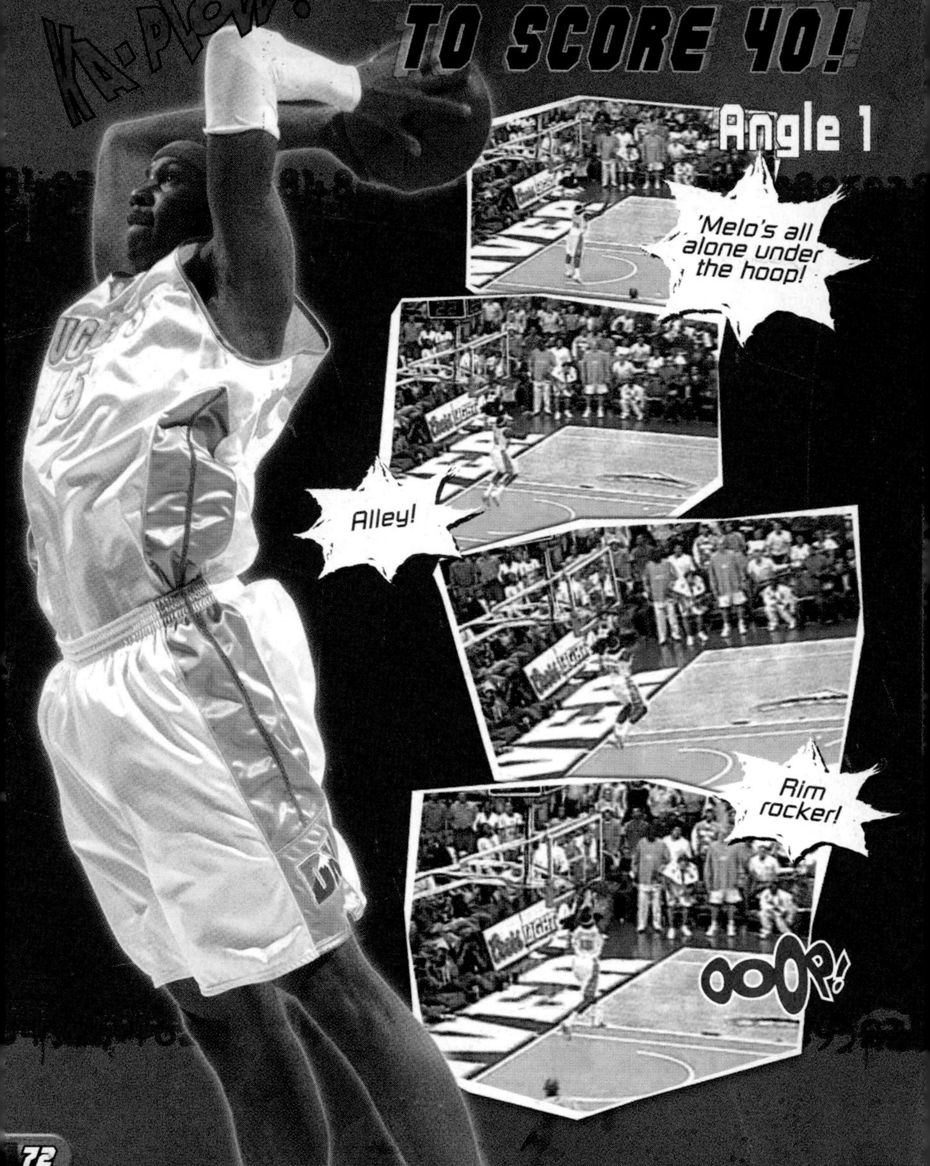
KA-PLOW!
Angle 1
'Melo's all alone under the hoop!
Alley!
Rim rocker!
OOOP!

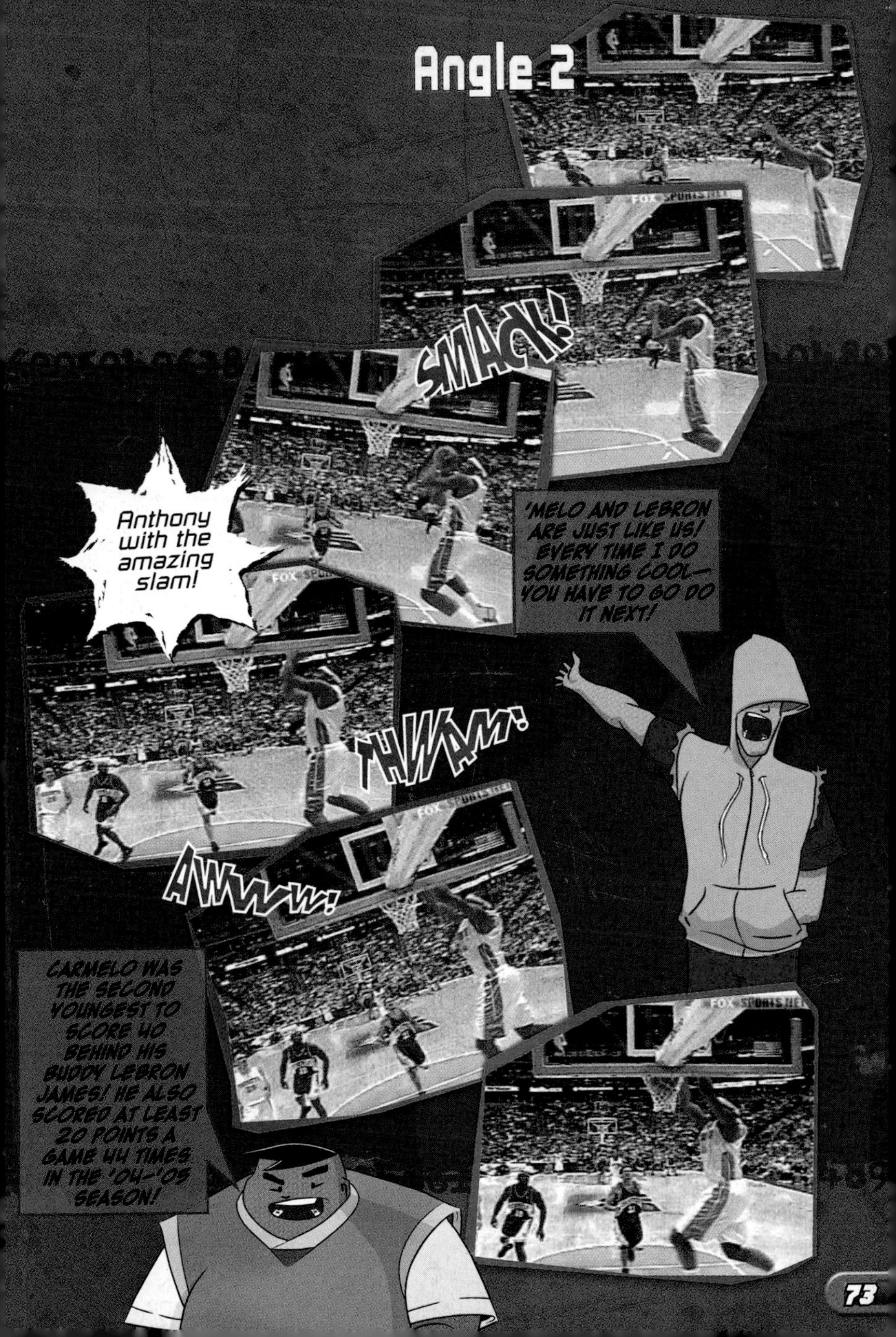
Angle 2
SMACK!
Anthony with the amazing slam!
'MELO AND LEBRON ARE JUST LIKE US! EVERY TIME I DO SOMETHING COOL— YOU HAVE TO GO DO IT NEXT!
THWAM!
AWWWW!
CARMELO WAS THE SECOND YOUNGEST TO SCORE 40 BEHIND HIS BUDDY LEBRON JAMES! HE ALSO SCORED AT LEAST 20 POINTS A GAME 44 TIMES IN THE '04-'05 SEASON!

SKILL #3//:

- GREAT PASS!

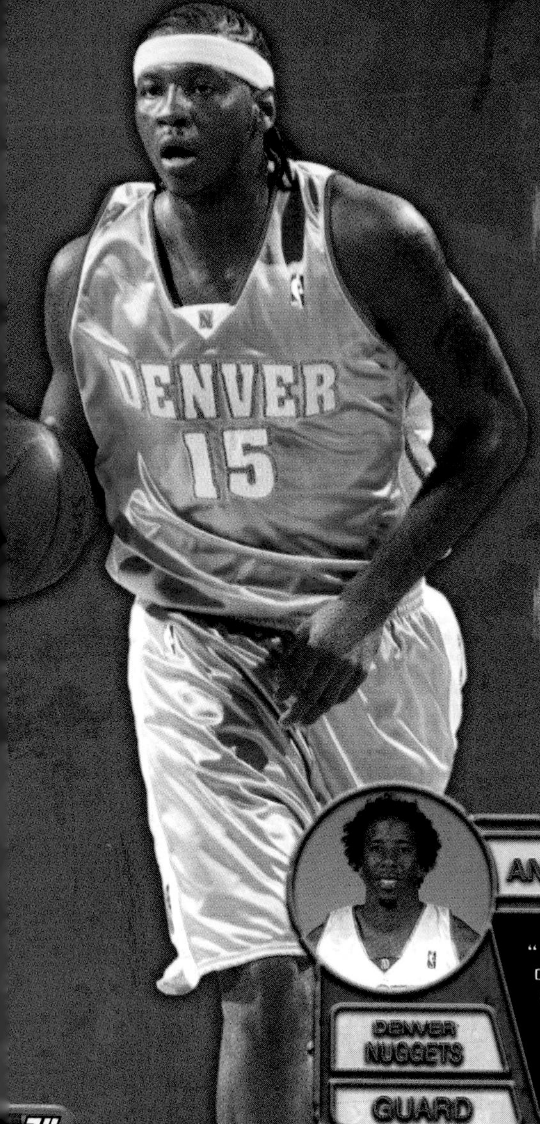

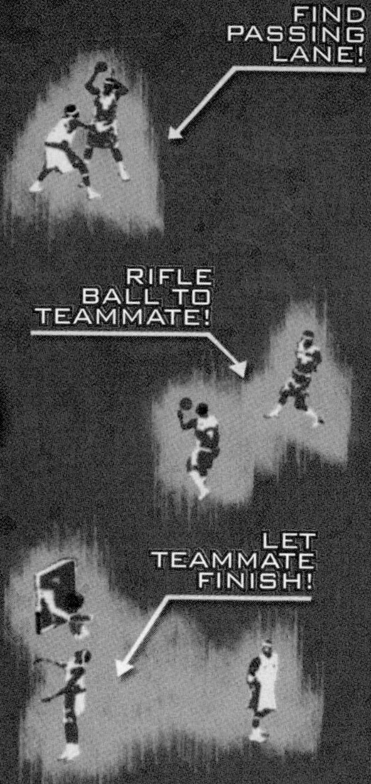

FIND PASSING LANE!
RIFLE BALL TO TEAMMATE!
LET TEAMMATE FINISH!

ANDRE MILLER

DENVER NUGGETS

GUARD

"THE THING THAT GIVES HIM AN EDGE IS THAT HE UNDERSTANDS HOW TO PLAY. MENTALLY HE PREPARES HIMSELF." [9]

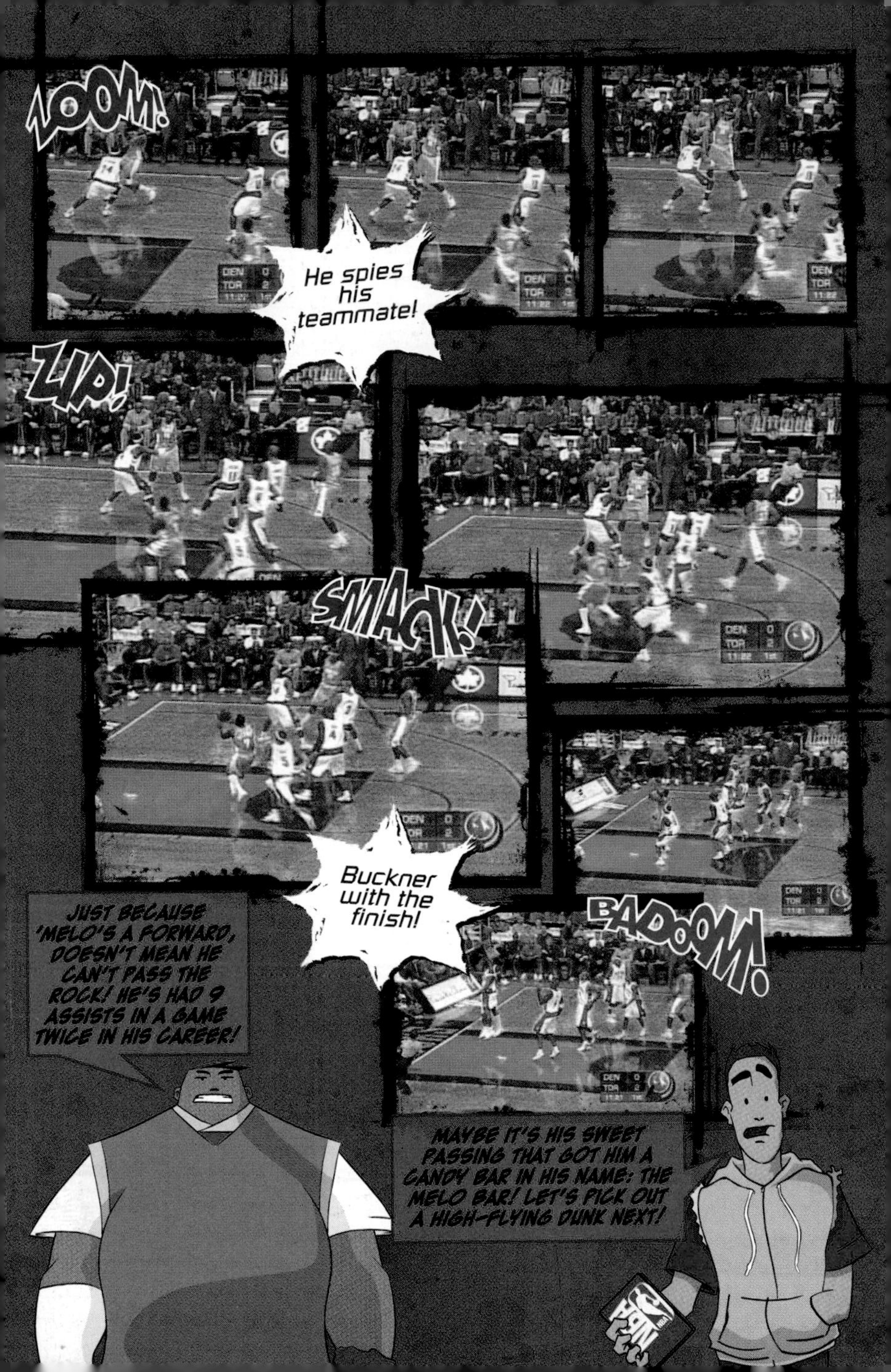
ZOOM!
He spies his teammate!
ZIP!
SMACK!
Buckner with the finish!
BADOOM!
JUST BECAUSE 'MELO'S A FORWARD, DOESN'T MEAN HE CAN'T PASS THE ROCK! HE'S HAD 9 ASSISTS IN A GAME TWICE IN HIS CAREER!
MAYBE IT'S HIS SWEET PASSING THAT GOT HIM A CANDY BAR IN HIS NAME: THE MELO BAR! LET'S PICK OUT A HIGH-FLYING DUNK NEXT!

SKILL #4//:
- GRAVITY-DEFYING DUNK!

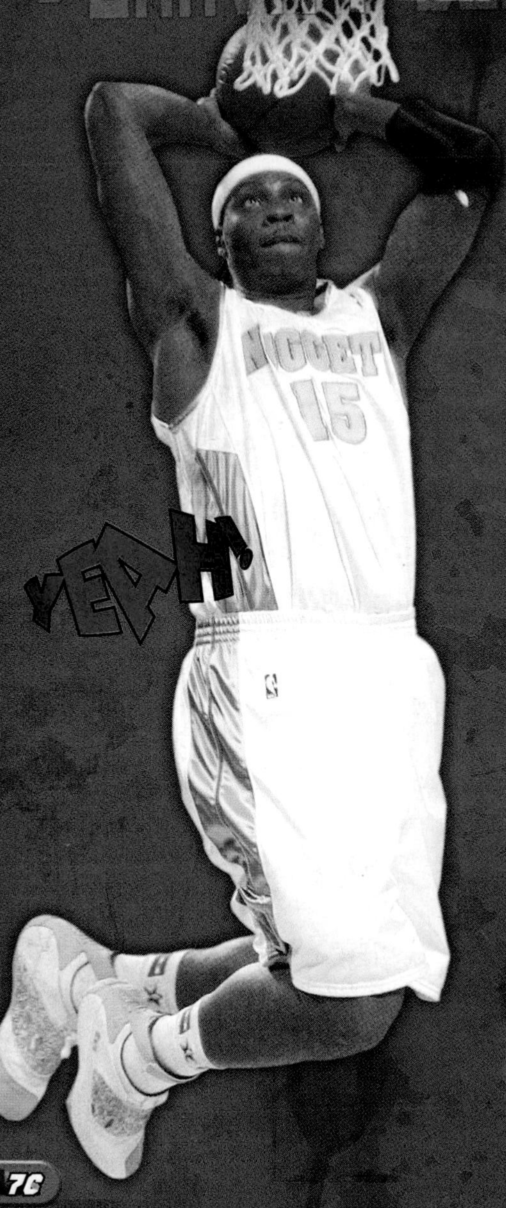
YEAH!
NUGGETS
15

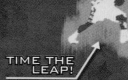

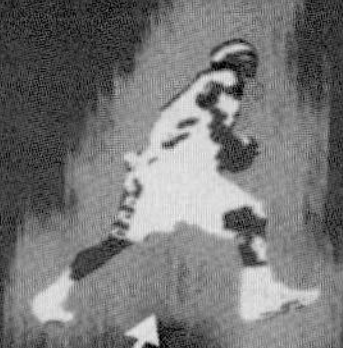
TIME THE LEAP!

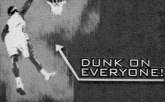

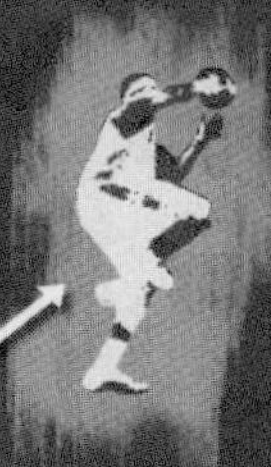
POUNCE OFF ONE FOOT!

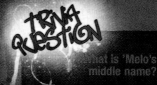

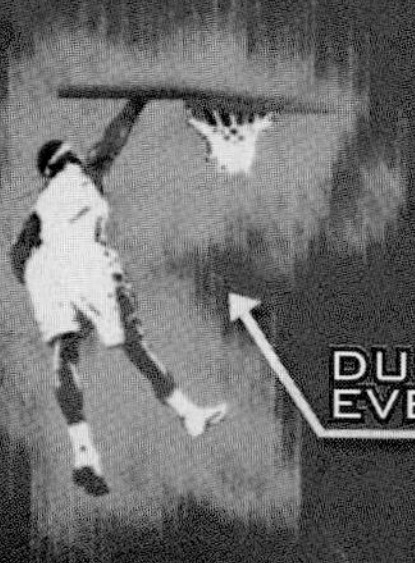
DUNK ON EVERYONE!

TRIVIA QUESTION

What is 'Melo's middle name?

Answer on page 91.

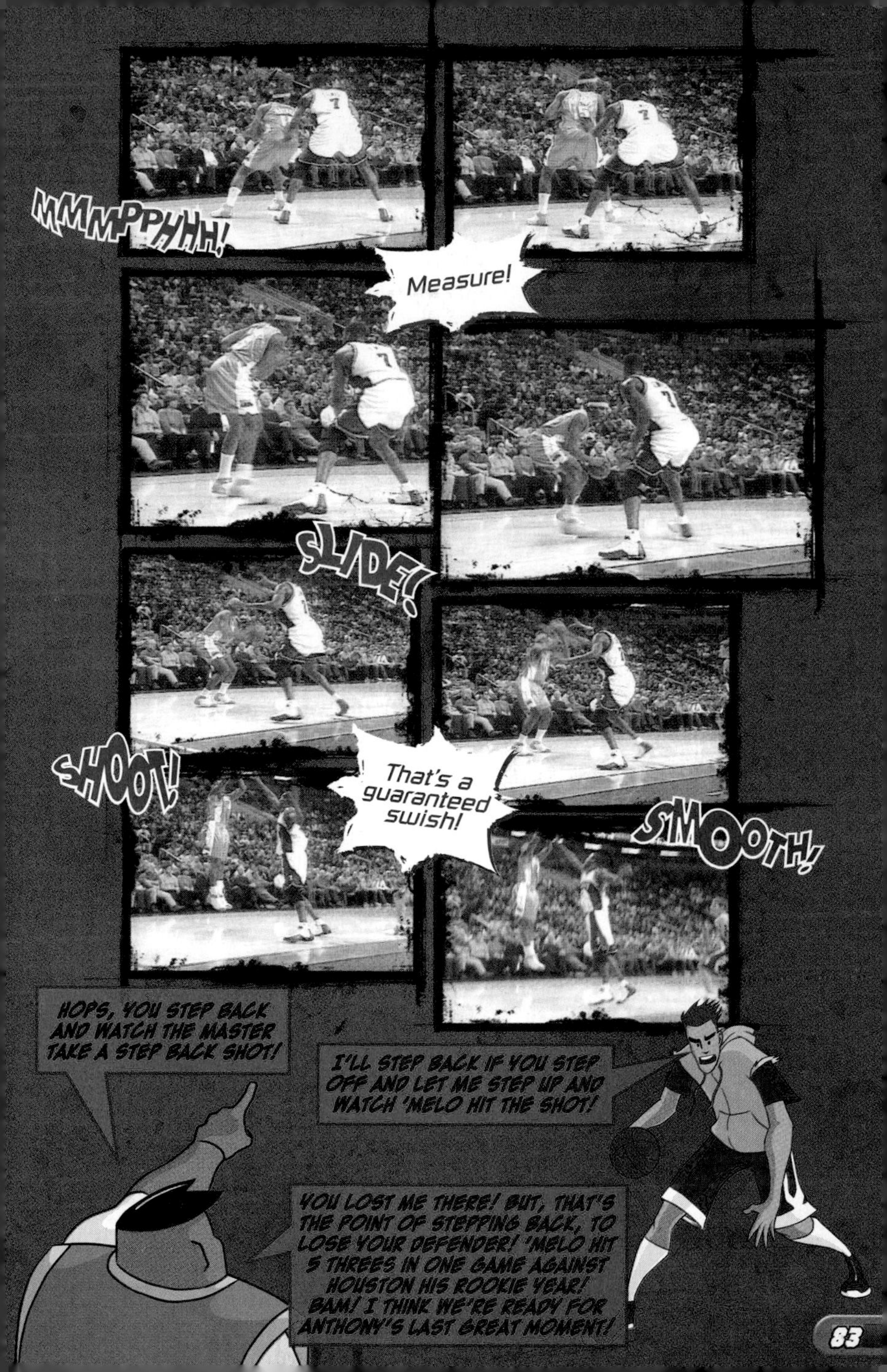
MMMPPHHH!
Measure!
SLIDE!
SHOOT!
That's a guaranteed swish!
SMOOTH!
HOPS, YOU STEP BACK AND WATCH THE MASTER TAKE A STEP BACK SHOT!
I'LL STEP BACK IF YOU STEP OFF AND LET ME STEP UP AND WATCH 'MELO HIT THE SHOT!
YOU LOST ME THERE! BUT, THAT'S THE POINT OF STEPPING BACK, TO LOSE YOUR DEFENDER! 'MELO HIT 5 THREES IN ONE GAME AGAINST HOUSTON HIS ROOKIE YEAR! BAM! I THINK WE'RE READY FOR ANTHONY'S LAST GREAT MOMENT!

GREAT MOMENT UNLOCKED!

2005 MVP OF ROOKIE-SOPHOMORE GAME!

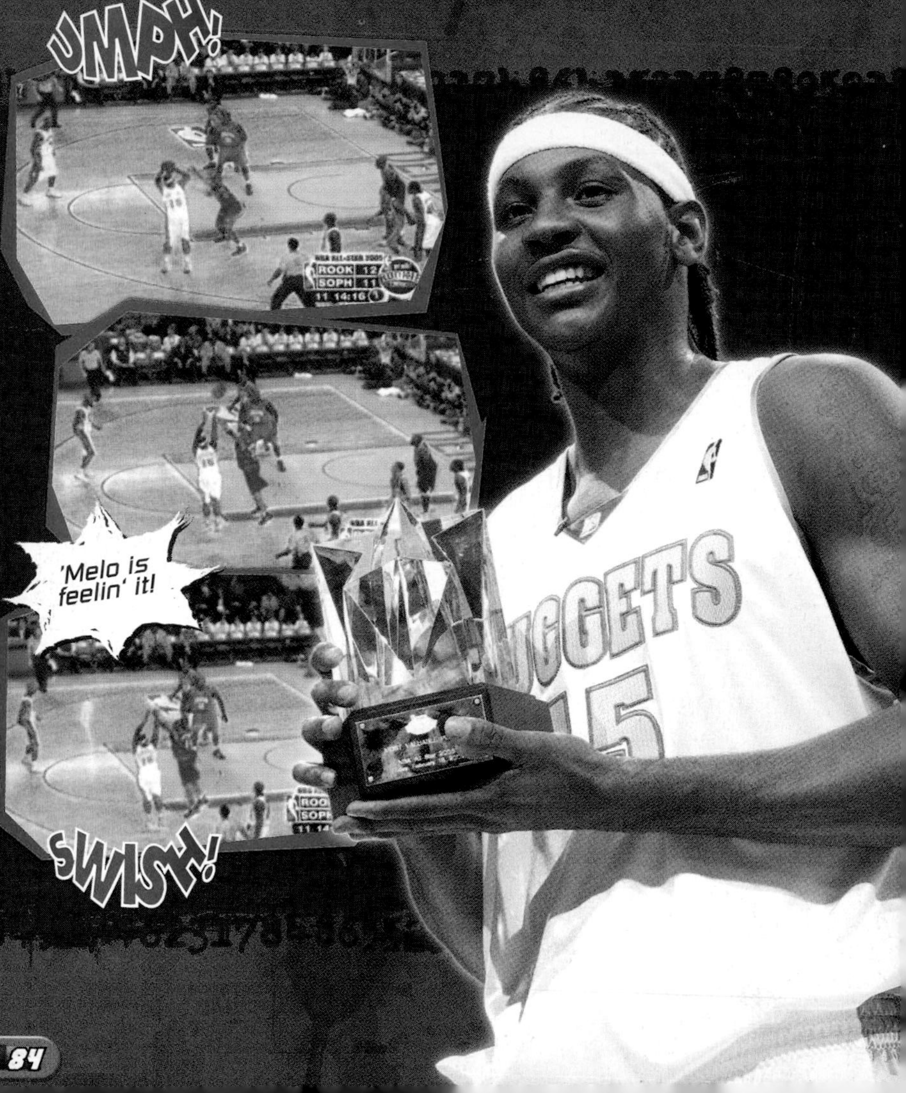
UMPH!
ROOK 12
SOPH 11
11 14:16
'Melo is feelin' it!
SWISH!
NUGGETS

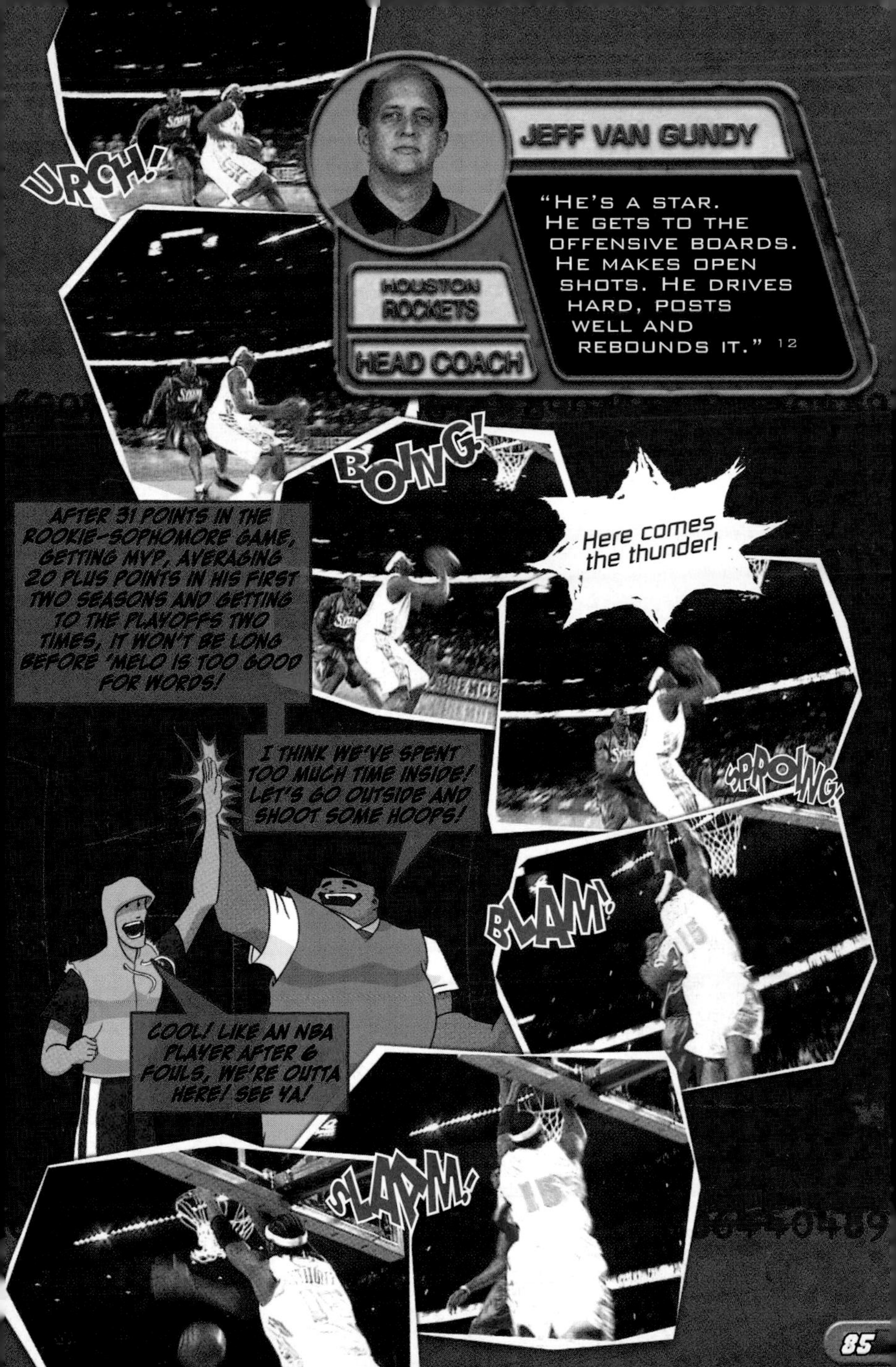
URCH!
JEFF VAN GUNDY
HOUSTON ROCKETS
HEAD COACH
"HE'S A STAR. HE GETS TO THE OFFENSIVE BOARDS. HE MAKES OPEN SHOTS. HE DRIVES HARD, POSTS WELL AND REBOUNDS IT." [12]
AFTER 31 POINTS IN THE ROOKIE-SOPHOMORE GAME, GETTING MVP, AVERAGING 20 PLUS POINTS IN HIS FIRST TWO SEASONS AND GETTING TO THE PLAYOFFS TWO TIMES, IT WON'T BE LONG BEFORE 'MELO IS TOO GOOD FOR WORDS!
BOING!
Here comes the thunder!
I THINK WE'VE SPENT TOO MUCH TIME INSIDE! LET'S GO OUTSIDE AND SHOOT SOME HOOPS!
SPROING!
BLAM!
COOL! LIKE AN NBA PLAYER AFTER 6 FOULS, WE'RE OUTTA HERE! SEE YA!
SLAM!

FOR THE BOOKS...

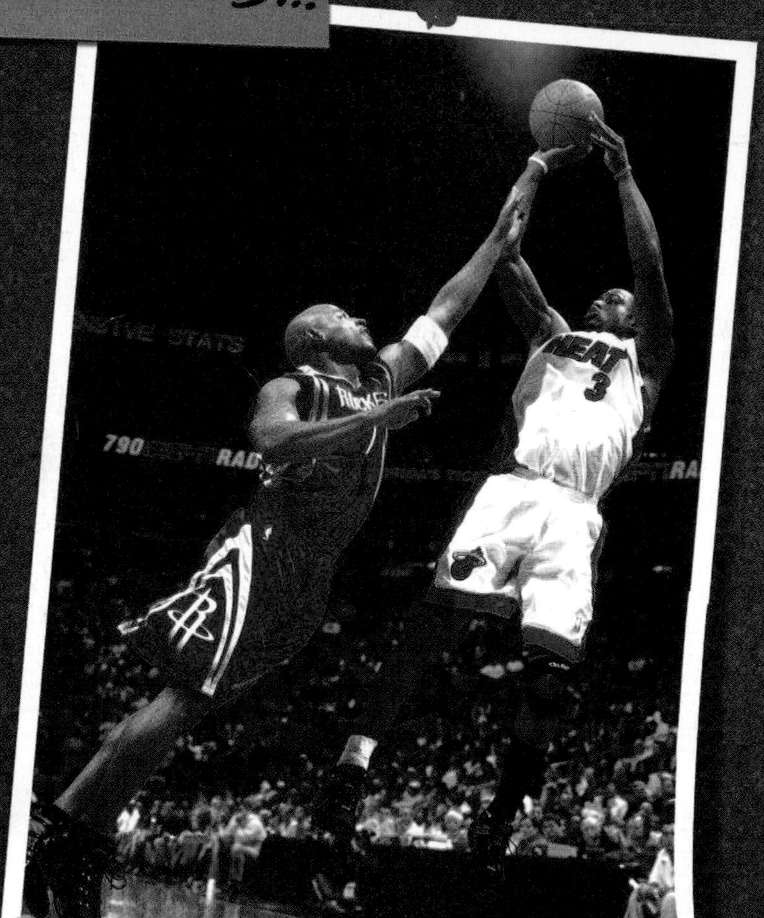

HEAT
3
790

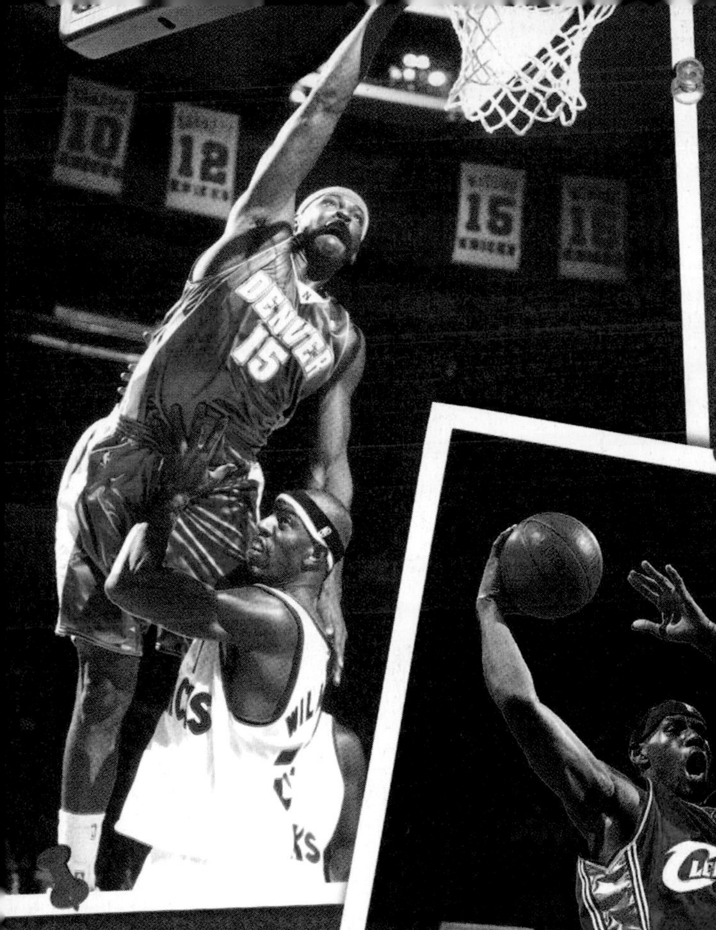
10
KNICKS
12
KNICKS
15
KNICKS
DENVER
15
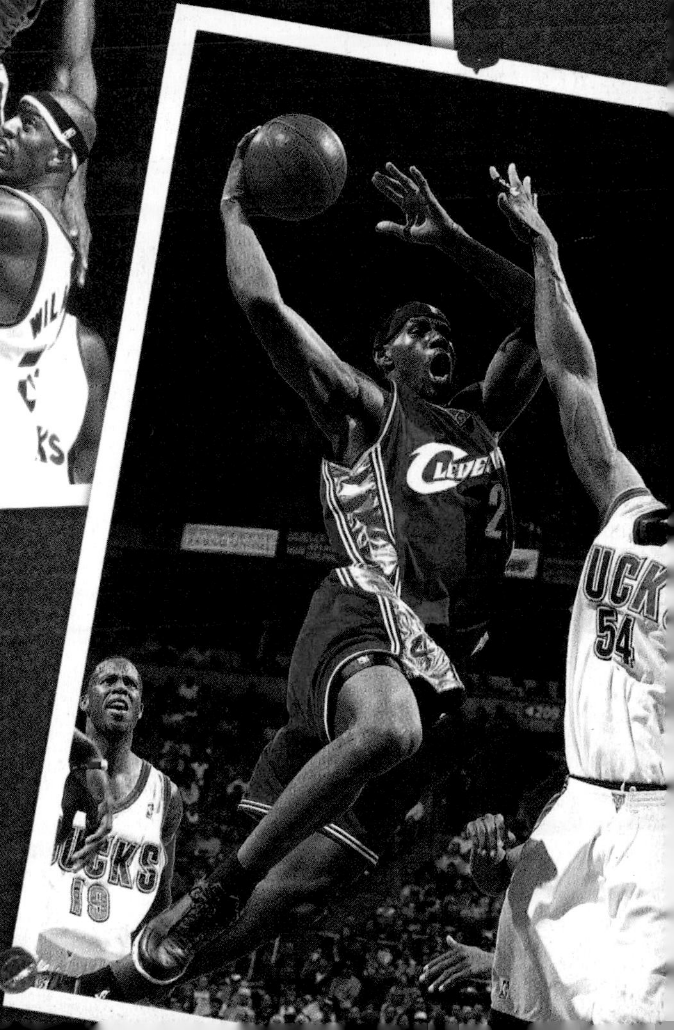
54
19

FUTURE STARS CAREER AVERAGES AND CAREER HIGHS!

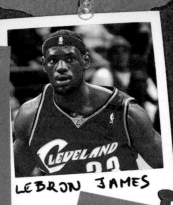

CAREER AVERAGES://

POINTS://	24.1
REBOUNDS://	6.4
ASSISTS://	6.6
STEALS://	1.93
MINUTES://	40.9

CAREER HIGHS://

POINTS://	56 @ Toronto 3/20/05
REBOUNDS://	18 vs. New York 4/14/05
ASSISTS://	15 vs. Memphis 1/26/05
STEALS://	7 @ Memphis 12/13/04
MINUTES://	55 vs. Memphis 11/29/03

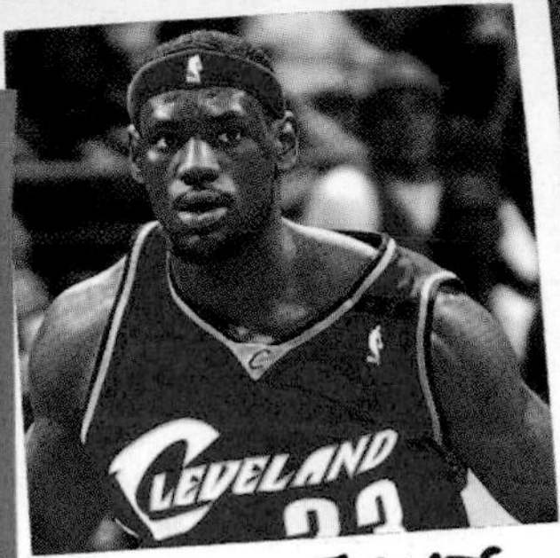
CLEVELAND

LEBRON JAMES

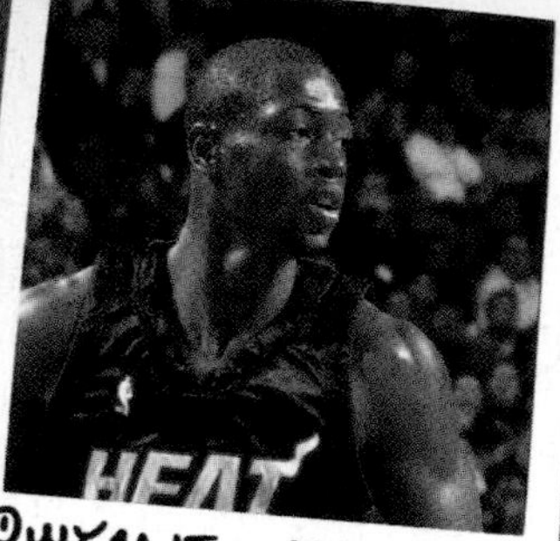
HEAT

DWYANE WADE

CAREER AVERAGES://

POINTS://	20.6
REBOUNDS://	4.7
ASSISTS://	5.8
STEALS://	1.5
MINUTES://	37

CAREER HIGHS://

POINTS://	48 @ Philadelphia 4/14/05
REBOUNDS://	10 - 5 times
ASSISTS://	12 - 3 times
STEALS://	6 vs New Orleans 3/16/04
MINUTES://	5 - 2 times

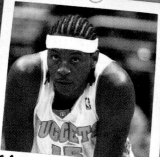

CAREER AVERAGES://

POINTS://	20.9
REBOUNDS://	5.9
ASSISTS://	2.7
STEALS://	1.05
MINUTES://	35.7

CAREER HIGHS://

POINTS://	41 vs. Seattle 3/30/04
REBOUNDS://	14 - 3 times
ASSISTS://	9 - 2 times
STEALS://	5 - 2 times
MINUTES://	46 - 2 times

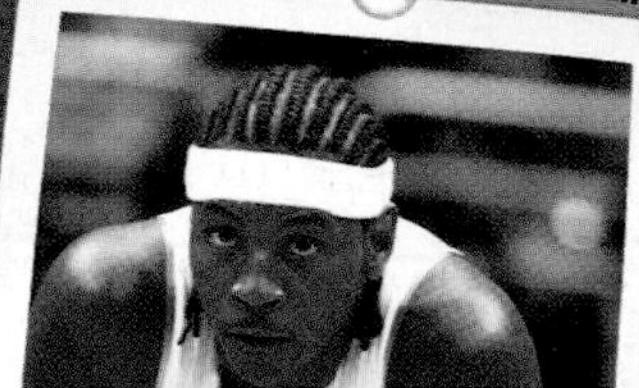

CARMELO ANTHONY

TREMENDOUS TOTALS
AFTER ONLY TWO SEASONS!

TOTALS://

GAMES://	159
POINTS://	3,829
REBOUNDS://	1,020
ASSISTS://	1,042
STEALS://	307
MINUTES://	6,510

LEBRON JAMES

TOTALS://

GAMES://	
POINTS://	138
REBOUNDS://	2,845
ASSISTS://	644
STEALS://	795
MINUTES://	207
	5,100

DWYANE WADE

TOTALS://

GAMES:	157
POINTS:	3,283
REBOUNDS:	924
ASSISTS:	421
STEALS:	165
MINUTES:	5,603

CARMELO ANTHONY

PHOTO CREDITS

Cover: Clockwise from Top Left: Jesse D. Garrabrant, Joe Murphy, Joe Murphy

Page 1: From Top: Gregory Shamus, Fernando Medina, Mitchell Layton
Page 3: Jesse D. Garrabrant
Page 4: From Left: Mitchell Layton, Victor Baldizon
Page 5: From Top: Ezra Shaw, Jesse D. Garrabrant
Page 8: Tim Defrisco
Page 9: From Top: Garrett Ellwood, Rocky Widner, Nathaniel S. Butler
Page 10: From Left: Mitchell Layton, David Liam Kyle
Page 11: From Left: Ezra Shaw, David Liam Kyle
Page 12: David Liam Kyle
Page 14: John Grieshop
Page 17: David Liam Kyle. Inset: NBAE
Page 18: David Liam Kyle
Page 20: Jesse D. Garrabrant
Page 24: Inset: Nathaniel S. Butler
Page 22: Kent Smith
Page 25: John Grieshop
Page 26: Garrett Ellwood. Inset: Gary Dineen
Page 28: Bill Baptist
Page 30: Nathaniel S. Butler
Page 32: Ron Turenne
Page 33: Ron Turenne
Page 35: Gary Dineen
Page 36: Ron Turenne
Page 38: Fernando Medina
Page 39: From Left: Layne Murdoch, Terrence Vaccaro
Page 40: Eliot J. Schechter
Page 42: Issac Baldizon. Inset: Victor Baldizon
Page 43: John Grieshop
Page 44: Issac Baldizon
Page 45: Jesse D. Garrabrant
Page 46: Scott Cunningham. Inset: Jeff Reinking
Page 48: Sam Forencich
Page 50: Glenn James. Inset: Jeff Reinking
Page 53: Victor Baldizon
Page 54: Issac Baldizon
Page 56: Jesse D. Garrabrant. Inset: Victor Baldizon
Page 58: Issac Baldizon
Page 60: Gary Dineen
Page 61: Andrew D. Bernstein
Page 62: Jesse D. Garrabrant
Page 63: Jesse D. Garrabrant
Page 64: From Left: Garrett Ellwood, Gregory Shamus
Page 65: From Left: Thearon Henderson, Joe Murphy
Page 66: Garrett Ellwood
Page 69: Inset: Ron Hoskins
Page 70: Nathaniel S. Butler
Page 72: Garrett Ellwood
Page 74: Bill Baptist. Inset: Michael Martin
Page 76: Ezra Shaw
Page 78: Rocky Widner. Inset: M. David Leeds
Page 81: Garrett Ellwood
Page 82: Noah Graham. Inset: Chris Graythen
Page 84: Andrew D. Bernstein
Page 85: Inset: Bill Baptist
Page 86: Fernando Medina
Page 87: Clockwise from Top Left: Nathaniel S. Butler, Gary Dineen
Page 88: From Top: Dan Lippitt/Allen Einstein, Glenn James, Andy Lyons
Page 89: From Top: Joe Murphy, Victor Baldizon, Brian Bahr

TOKYOPOP THANKS:// JOHN HAREAS AND MICHAEL LEVINE OF THE NBA

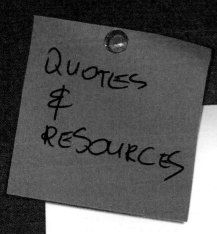

QUOTES & RESOURCES

1. David Dupree, "James and Co. Ready to Fill Shoes of Jordan and Co.,"
USA Today, February 16, 2005.
2. Ibid.
3. Sean Deveney, "Crystal Baller," December 13, 2004, Sporting News,
http://www.sportingnews.com/exclusives/20041213/586329.html.
4. Steve Kyler, "One-on-One with Dwyane Wade," February 15, 2005, Hoopsworld,
http://www.hoopsworld.com/printer_7239.shtml.
5. "Postgame Quotes," January 3, 2005, NBA.com,
http://www.nba.com/sonics/news/quotes050103.html
6. Ibid.
7. Jill Lieber, "Heat Star Wade-ing Into Special Territory,"
USA Today, February 17, 2005.
8. "Carmelo Anthony – Rookie of the Year," NBA.com, (accessed June 28, 2005),
http://www.nba.com/nuggets/news/carmelo_anthony_theroy.html.
9. Ibid.
10. Ibid.
11. Ibid.
12. Ibid.

TRIVIA ANSWERS

Pg. 18: Tiger Woods
Pg. 33: The Hornets
Pg. 37: 55 minutes vs. Memphis
Pg. 45: 15
Pg. 53: Chicken and Mashed Potatoes

Pg. 58: Shaq
Pg. 76: Kyan
Pg. 80: 5 vs. Houston 12/26/03

TOKYOPOP

UNCANNY

ALLEN IVERSON

GREATEST STARS OF THE NBA: A CINE-MANGA SLAM DUNK!

GREATEST STARS OF THE NBA

Collect the Series!

A
ALL AGES

www.TOKYOPOP.com

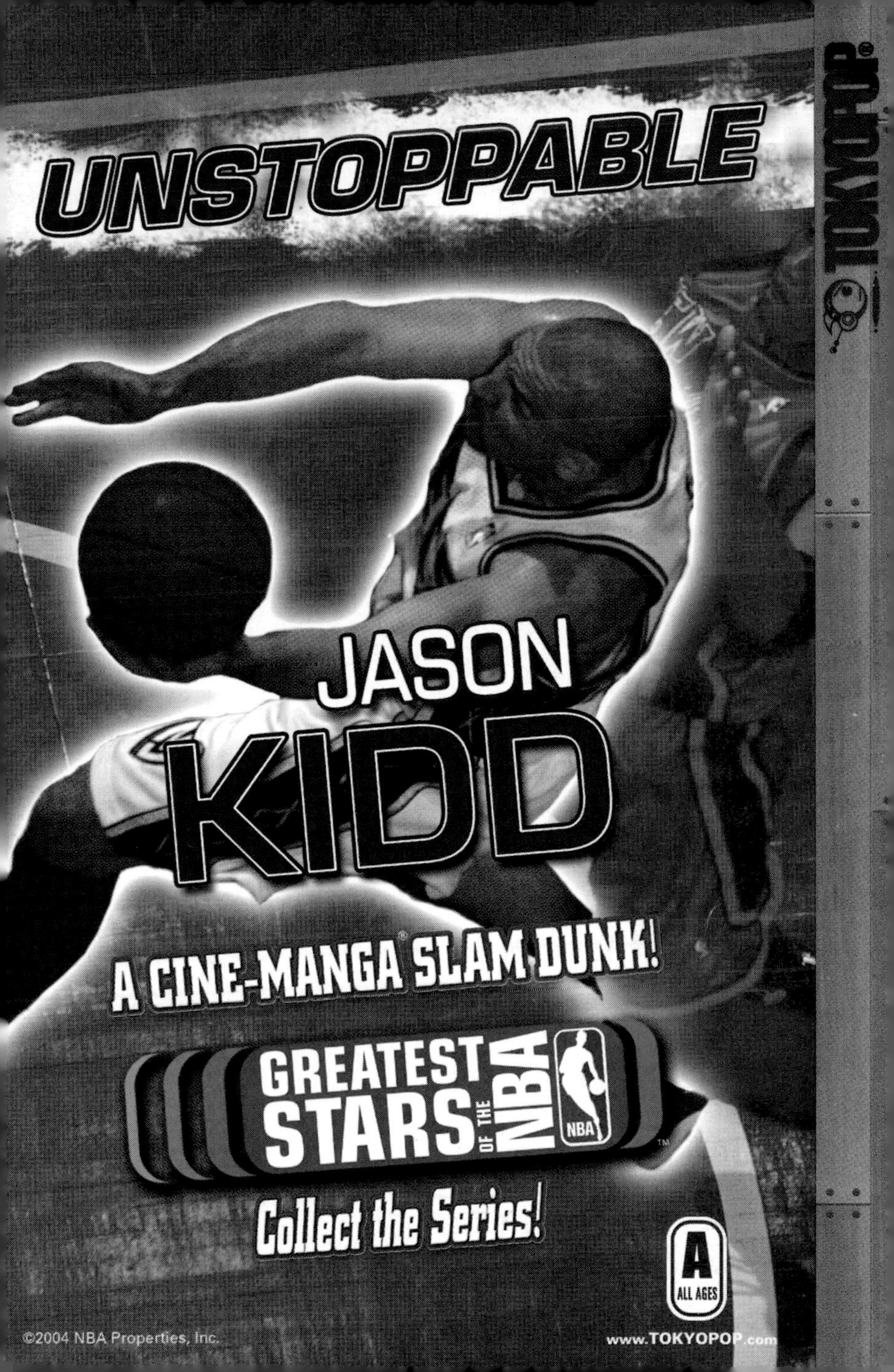
TOKYOPOP
UNSTOPPABLE
JASON
KIDD
A CINE-MANGA SLAM DUNK!
GREATEST STARS OF THE NBA
NBA
Collect the Series!
A
ALL AGES
©2004 NBA Properties, Inc.
www.TOKYOPOP.com

ALSO AVAILABLE FROM 🐾TOKYOPOP®

MANGA

10.19.04Y